ROMAN

NORTH

AFRICA

To all the family
and in particular those
who came with me long ago
on the memorable journey from
Gabes to Gafsa
and Tozeur

ROMAN

NORTH AFRICA

E. Lennox Manton

Seaby

LONDON

© E. Lennox Manton 1988
First published 1988

Typeset by Servis Filmsetting Ltd, Manchester
and printed and bound in Great Britain
by Anchor Brendon Ltd
Tiptree, Essex
for the publishers
B.A. Seaby Ltd
8 Cavendish Square
London W1M 0AJ

Distributed by
B.T. Batsford Ltd
P.O. Box 4, Braintree, Essex CM7 7QY

Manton, Lennox
    Roman North Africa.
    1. Africa. North Africa, to ca. 440
    I. Title
    939'.7

ISBN 1-85264-007-3

Contents

Illustrations

Preface

From ancient times to the present day North Africa has been the scene of several crucial battles. The defeat of Hannibal at Zama in 202 BC was one turning point in history, and the Allied victory at El Alamein in 1942 was another. The virtual destruction of the Carthaginian nation by Scipio in the Third Punic War can, in a way, be compared with the Jewish Holocaust brought about by Hitler in Nazi Germany.

After the fall of Carthage, North Africa developed into a wealthy Roman province. The remains of the cities, the mosaics and the art treasures that have been recovered and are now preserved in museums, attest to a sophisticated and pleasant way of life enjoyed by the majority of those who settled in the country. Though there were some internecine wars with the indigenous Berber tribes, the peace-keeping efforts of the Third Augustan Legion and the expertise of their engineers contributed to maintaining this way of life in the first and second centuries AD.

The schism and the periodic violence between the Catholics and the Donatists in later years has its echoes in Northern Ireland today. The Vandals and the Arabs finally brought down the Roman culture and replaced it with that of Muhammed which flourishes today, and this obliterated the vast achievements of the Romans which were soon forgotten and fell into oblivion.

I must thank in no small measure both my daughter Sarah and Brian Skelley for their invaluable help in producing a draft from a hand which I have been told is more suitable for writing prescriptions. I must also thank my son Gavin for allowing me to photograph and illustrate the coins of Cyrene and those commemorating Hadrian's visit to North Africa, both from the stock of B.A. Seaby Ltd. The maps of North Africa and of Tunisia were produced by Alan Miles of Cartodraftech; the plans of Leptis Magna, Sabratha, Thuburbo Maius, Carthage and Dougga are reproduced by courtesy of Swan Hellenic Ltd from their Handbook, and the Piazza Armerina mosaic through the kindness of Peter Clayton.

To David Norden-Angus I express my great appreciation for the pleasant hours we spent in his darkroom producing the prints, and for his enthusiasm and valuable suggestions. I must also not forget Rosemary Bradley and Peter Clayton for their patience and guidance in editing and John Henderson, who always managed to turn up a reference out of a vast library which he has stored in his roof. Lastly, but by no means least, my indebtedness to the Director of the Institut National d'Archeologie et d'Art in the Place du Château in Tunis is very evident, as it is also to the Director of the Bardo Museum, for allowing me to take and to publish the necessary photographs, and to the administrative staff for their kind help.

E. Lennox Manton
Guildford 1988

1

North Africa and the Deserts today

Some thirty years ago, Dame Rose Macaulay wrote on *The Pleasure of Ruins*. To the Italian artists of the eighteenth century they were a nostalgic theme to be included in landscapes, to the archaeologist they can conceal a secret that only his expertise can unravel, but to many they are merely heaps of stones, often overgrown with weeds and scrub and in general a very dull sort of affair. However, throughout the world, and in the Middle East and North Africa in particular, the imposing remains of ancient monuments and cities can evoke awe and wonder at the achievements of those who peopled them in centuries past. These ruins have often been rediscovered by dedicated travellers such as J.L. Buckhardt, who, dressed as an arab, was the first European to see Petra in Jordan on 22 August 1812. At that time, his travels were largely treated as the product of a fertile imagination.

In North Africa one can see many of the best preserved cities of the Roman world. Though their treasures have been sadly pillaged and many of their marble columns removed – to grace the Great Mosque of Kairouan (*Ill. 1*), not to mention those that have found their way to Virginia Water in Surrey and the 660 that are now in the Palace of Versailles – sufficient remain. Their stones and walls glow in the evening light, casting soft shadows that creep over the empty streets. The heavy silence is broken only by the rustle of a soft breeze or a rattling outburst of cicadas. In the dusk the figure of a local peasant may cross the forum to his village nearby, often built from the city's stones, and the ruins stand sentinel to a past heritage.

The Hamites were the first dominant settlers to discover North Africa, beginning their occupation around 4500 BC; the first of subsequent invasions by the Phoenicians, Greeks, Romans, Vandals, then the Byzantines and, finally, the Arabs. Almost finally, that is, for the Napoleonic armies invaded the country in the late eighteenth century and their relatively transient presence left its mark in the continued use of the French language and legal system, the Napoleonic Code.

Once the Hamites had discovered the art of agriculture they spread

1 *Kairouan was founded by Oqba ibn Nafi in* AD *671 and the Great Mosque was built shortly afterwards, using materials taken from a number of the ancient ruined cities nearby. A particular feature is the vast number and different designs of the re-used Roman column capitals. Kairouan is a Muslim holy city, the third holiest in Islam after Mecca and Medineh.*

over the fertile regions of Cyrenaica and Tripolitania, reaching out north-west to Numidia and Mauritania, present-day Tunisia, Algeria and Morocco, an area which is known as the Maghreb (*Ill. 2*). The wooded and hospitable regions of the far west, with a reliable rainfall, are separated from the inhospitable deserts of the South by the Aures mountains of Algeria and the Atlas of Morocco. Beyond these mountain ranges, the country gradually gives way to the beautiful landscapes of the

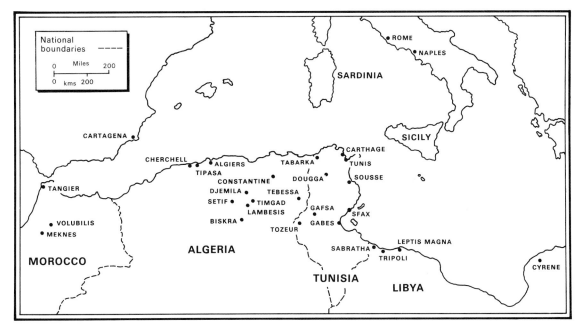

2 Roman North Africa.

pre-Sahara, thence to the oases of the desert such as Erfoud, Biskra and El Oued, and in southern Tunisia, Nefta and Tozeur together with many others to the east and south. It is these southern oases that border the great rolling Ergs of the Sahara, in infinite shades of yellow and gold, everchanging with the shifting sun.

Well to the south in Algeria are the oases of Quarglia and El Golea, which itself borders on to the Great Erg Occidental; still further south are the plateaux and canyons, the palm groves and the valleys of the Tassili. This area adjoins the dry and difficult terrain of the Hoggar, an inhospitable country to the European, but home to the tall proud Tuareg tribes.

In southern Tunisia, Nefta and Tozeur lie close to the Algerian border not far from the southern perimeter of the great Chott Djerid. This expanse is in reality the vast dried-up salt beds of erstwhile lakes and lagoons, ringed around with a series of small oases; a hazardous terrain to cross. Larger oases dot the desert from the Nile to the coast. One hundred and fifty miles across the desert to the north of Wadi Halfa, which was once on the Egyptian border with the Sudan but now lies under the waters of Lake Nasser, is the Oasis of Selima. It is a small water hole surrounded by a few struggling date palms and lies in a depression amongst the dunes, but once in times long past it was an important staging post on the original slave route from Nubia to Egypt.

Futher to the west is Uweinat, a stark high granite outcrop that rises suddenly from the flat desert, with a welcome cool spring in a deep shady cleft in the rock. Much further on is Kufra and, nearer to Alexandria, in the Western Desert lies Siwa. These two are amongst the largest. A little south of Kufra and east of Uweinat is the Plateau of the Gilf, 1200 metres high; here at its base one can often find the artefacts, stone hand axes and arrow-heads, left by Stone Age man. The oases show the locations where a deep undergound water table, which extends well into Central Africa, comes near to the surface to produce these havens in the emptiness.

The deserts are not a featureless expanse, but contain many varieties of landscape. Outcrops of granite, some with pinnacles covered with white guana, mark the resting place of migratory birds on their journey south; and in the shade of the rocks are often the remnants of rudimentary nests, some with deserted eggs, but no sign of a dead body. The course of the ancient wadis, their steep banks hundreds of metres apart, give on to endless sandy plains, which are broken up here and there by little heaps of stony excrescences, as if the whole area had bubbled and boiled and been frozen in the process. Other tracts are so flat that they extend to the horizon where the red sun sinks to ground level, casting long thin shadows which quickly fade into the sudden night, a night lit up by a canopy of stars; it is almost like standing in the middle of a plate. The temperature drops dramatically and the only noise comes from the subdued clatter of the cook, the hiss of the pressure lamp, and the murmuring of companions.

The great sand dune barrier crosses the sandy plain at the very north and rolls away from the east to the great Ergs of the Sahara, countless miles to the west like a broad rippling and undulating backbone, windswept with the whirling eddies of light brown sand. After some miles, the switchback of the dunes gives way to further expanses of small coarse stones and shallow valleys until the welcome green palms of Kufra come into view, stretching away as far as the horizon. The markets in the oasis are a polyglot. Women bargain for the vegetables and spices, dressed in bright, bold-patterned voluminous garments, sometimes with large brass rings dangling from their ear lobes. The thin sheep that graze on the nearby plateau of the Gilf wander about under the feet of the nomads. Bales of brilliant cloth are stacked into piles in a dark shop, whilst heaps of gaily japanned buckets and bowls are spread about on the ground in front of the vendor.

Barter still prevails. Tins of tea are exchanged for fresh eggs in the tent of 'The Chef de L'Oasis', a ritual that extends over many elaborately prepared cups of coffee. Finally the deal is complete. The tea is handed over with due ceremony and the eggs taken away carefully arranged in a basket. The caravans that still bring these commodities to the oasis call to mind the Garamantes of old who came to Leptis further to the west: only now we are dealing not only in spices and cloths, but in buckets, baskets and other commodities of the present day.

It is these peoples, together with the Berbers of Algeria and Morocco, often more rounded in feature than the Arabs, who have replaced those early Hamites. The Berbers still speak their own language and inhabit their villages in the Aures Mountains, and those villages in the Todro Gorges and the valleys of the Dra beyond the Atlas. All had to come to terms in the past with the succession of invaders: the Phoenicians, the Greeks and Romans, the Vandals, Arabs, the Turks and, finally, the French.

2

Punic Carthage and the Carthaginians

The Greeks and the Minoans from Crete were amongst the earliest maritime peoples of the Mediterranean. The Minoans before 1500 BC had a brisk trade with Egypt. At Tell El-Amarna, the new capital built by the Pharaoh Akhenaten, who has become one of the great enigmas of the Eighteenth Dynasty, Sir Flinders Petrie discovered a shop containing a quantity of Minoan decorated pottery, an import valued by the Egyptians.

The Phoenicians at this time were living cheek by jowl with the Canaanites. They were in possession of the coastal strip of Palestine and the Levant, being chiefly settled around the then unimportant city of Tyre. They had discovered the minerals of the Spanish peninsula and their early ships, those of Tarshish of the Old Testament, had passed the Pillars of Hercules (Gibraltar) to reach Tartessus on the Spanish Atlantic coast. The journey in those days took several months there and back, for the ships were small and hugged the coast, but by 825 BC, as a result of their business acumen, the Phoenicians had become the main trading nation in the Mediterranean and Tyre had become an important centre. They had developed into a national 'East India Company', solely preoccupied with import and export. To protect their trade routes they opened up small colonies and landfalls along the North African coast, mostly to the west of Libya. These acted as places of refuge from the Mediterranean storms, as ship's chandlers, and as trading posts to deal in the ivory and the other goods that the caravans brought to the coast from Central Africa. The anchorages had to be sympathetic to their relatively fragile wooden ships, so the natural rocky harbours had to be avoided and hence the rugged coast of Cyrenaica, later exploited by the Greeks, was not popular. The few sandy shores were sought out and became the site of towns such as Utica and Djerba in the Gulf of Garbes.

Utica was one of the most important ports from earliest times, being concerned with the tin trade, and the last port of call before Gibraltar. It lay at the estuary of the great Mejerda river, which unhappily brought down vast quantities of alluvial deposit from the fertile expanses of country along its course. Over the years this forced the sea to retreat, thus destroying the function of the city as a port, and today it lies as much as five miles inland from the coast. The island of Djerba was the reputed land of the Lotus Eaters, where Ulysses spent an indolent period of his life with the tribes of the Lotophagi. The Phoenicians, who were far from indolent, joined the island to the mainland by a causeway, which was later rebuilt by the Romans, and they harvested the very extensive beds of the murex shellfish which flourished in the Gulf. The purple dye extracted from them was one of their chief exports, but enormous quantities had to be gathered to produce only a small amount of the dye.

Beds of murex were also to be found along the coast around Tyre and these too were harvested. Because of its rich colour and rarity, the dye was in great demand throughout the Roman world, and was reserved for the garments of the Imperial family and the aristocracy. A purple stripe on the white toga of a senator denoted the rank of magistrate. The murex remained the only source of the colour until it was accidentally produced chemically in Victorian times, and became the first of the aniline dyes.

The Phoenicians spread their colonies to Malta and Cadiz, as well as to their nearest and most important footholds in Sicily, which were later destined to become the cause of most of their subsequent troubles and wars. No written records remain of this period, so that the actual date of the founding of Carthage is not known. However, the Athenian historian Timaeus gives a date of 814 BC, which he possibly derived from the sources which were then available.

The legend of Dido is well known. She was Elissa, a princess of Tyre, and married to Acherbas, whose wealth was envied by her brother Pygmalion of Tyre. She fled to North Africa from Tyre after Pygmalion had murdered her husband, taking in her retinue a number of temple priestesses. It was common practice in the various Syrian religious rites for the priestesses to take part in ritual prostitution, which still prevailed in Greek and Roman times. In fact Corinth, which was the most prosperous city in Greece in the sixth century BC, had a magnificent temple dedicated to Aphrodite, the goddess of love, on the summit of precipitous Acro-Corinth. It overlooked the city and its harbours and was served by over a thousand priestess prostitutes, who were famous and known throughout the ancient world as 'The Corinthian Girls'. The title smacks somewhat of a chorus line in a revue.

The harbours of Corinth were eventually packed with Phoenician ships, many from Carthage and the Levant, together with those from Egypt and, ultimately, Rome. The climb of 600 metres to the Temple of Aphrodite was a well trodden and exhausting one, no doubt even more so after the temple rituals had been completed. Saint Paul, when in Corinth, endeavoured to point out to the citizens the error of their ways, but he only succeeded in provoking a riot. One thing is quite certain; the temple maidens of Dido would have had little objection to founding a new colony at the end of the road.

Having decided on the future site of Carthage, Dido bought from the local tribe of the Maxitane, the amount of land that could be enclosed with the hide of an ox. Her followers cunningly cut the largest hide they could obtain into very thin strips, which were laid end to end, and thus managed to enclose the Byrsa Hill together with an area of beach for a bridgehead. By this manoeuvre they established the boundaries of the first settlement, building their first citadel on the Byrsa Hill, named after *byrsa*, Greek for oxhide. It is quite possible that she rejeted Utica as a capital realizing that the port facilities were already in jeopardy from the silt brought down by the Mejerda river. In the main, Syrian women were very capable and astute; during the Severan Dynasty of Rome, it was more often than not the Syrian princesses who were the power behind the Emperors.

The death of Dido is as legendary as the founding of Carthage. According to Virgil, the Trojan hero Aeneas escaped from Troy with his father Anchises and his son, to wander the Mediterranean. Blown off course, he landed in Carthage where he indulged in an amorous dalliance with the Queen. Eventually tiring of the relationship he departed to found Rome, whereupon the inconsolable Dido did away with herself. The dates of the founding of Carthage and the fall of Troy do not tie up by several hundred years, so this account should be treated sceptically. Another legend suggests that Dido committed suicide to escape the attentions of Iarbus, the King of the local Numidian tribe who sold her the oxhide.

Whatever the truth of the matter, Carthage was founded and became the greatest and wealthiest city on the North African coast for four hundred years. In time, the city extended beyond its original boundaries into gardens, rich villas and areas of cultivation which supplied the city markets. From 700 BC, the Greeks were also infiltrating the Mediterranean coasts and islands and setting up colonies. They had established themselves not only in Asia Minor but also in southern Italy, and the remains of their early cities can be seen in Sicily today. This development worried the Carthaginians and in 550 BC, they sent an expeditionary force to Sicily to protect their nationals, but in 480 BC the protracted and intermittent skirmishing erupted into the battle of Himera in which the Carthaginians were defeated and thrown out by the Greeks. Now unable to protect their valuable trade routes, their lucrative import and export business vanished. The end of the fifth century BC was a time of austerity, which was reflected in their tombs and also in their hatred for the Greeks. As often in times of stress, the priests became an authoritative force in the community and the rituals of child sacrifice to the national deities were firmly established, much to the disgust of the neighbouring peoples across the Mediterranean and elsewhere.

The advance of Nebuchadnezzar on Syria and Palestine, which ended in the fall of Tyre in 574 BC, had caused panic among the Phoenicians of the coastal towns, who emigrated in droves to the Punic towns of North Africa before their capital fell to the invader. Carthage especially was affected by an influx of refugees, so that the Carthaginians themselves were forced to neglect their trade and increase their agriculture, for in the past they had imported the greater part of their food. They spread further into Tunisia to the regions of Sousse and Garbes, and spent the next hundred years developing their new-found talents. But it was the local native farmers who suffered most. Many were driven into the less viable hinterland and into the mountains, whilst the wealthier Carthaginians organised the better land into large agricultural estates, growing fruit and raising cattle, quite often employing those whose holdings they had absorbed.

Over the succeeding years their agriculture progressed to the extent that, at the end of the fourth century BC, Diodorus Siculus remarked on the orchards of fruit trees, the pomegranates and the figs, which were watered by extensive conduits. He also noted the luxurious houses, full barns and the fields of cattle, sheep and horses; but their final success story was in bee-keeping, in which they excelled. The production of honey soon became another flourishing industry, for honey was used in place of sugar which was not known as such in the ancient world. The wax of the comb, known as Punic Wax, was also a valuable side-line and was exported in quantity to Italy, where it was greatly prized by the Romans for medicinal purposes.

A work on agronomy which extended to twenty-eight volumes was written by Mago, a Carthaginian, in the third century BC. Although the original has been lost, its contents have been extensively quoted by later Latin writers. He lays down detailed principles, including the advice that olive trees, which they introduced, should be planted in groves, twenty-five metres apart. Extensive groves planted in this way can be seen today near Djerba and Gabes, and elsewhere in southern Tunisia, more methodical in fact than many of the groves in southern Spain. Apart from the olive and the vine, the date palm was also brought into cultivation and became the city emblem of Carthage (*Ill. 3*).

3 *Silver tetradrachm of Carthage, fourth century BC. The reverse shows the date palm, the emblem of Carthage.*

The Lord Julius mosaic of the late fourth century AD, discovered near the Byrsa Hill in Carthage (now in the Bardo Museum in Tunis), illustrates in detail the life on one of these later wealthy estates. At the bottom of the mosaic the owner of the estate is pictured seated enthroned on a chair and surrounded by his servants. In the opposite corner stands his wife, splendidly dressed with an elaborate coiffure and a very self-satisfied expression on her face as her maid-servant hands her a very costly necklace, taken from a jewel box that she has clasped tightly to her bosom (*Ill. 4*).

The poor indigenous farmer, who had been driven further inland, was left to grow what he could on more difficult land. A tenth of his produce had to be given in tax to Carthage, a proportion that was often raised arbitrarily to well above the statutory limit. By now they had developed the small Phoenician colonies in Tripolitania into the cities of Leptis Magna, Oea and Sabratha, and had taken full advantage of the trade brought in by the caravans of the Garamantes. They did not, however, penetrate east of the Libyan border into Cyrenaica, which remained loyal to the Greek tradition.

Hanno was perhaps the most famous Carthaginian admiral. Very early in the fifth century BC he explored the west coast of Africa, reaching the

4 *Detail from the 'Lord Julius' mosaic showing the richly dressed mistress of the estate being handed a necklace by her maid-servant from a jewel box. Late fourth century AD. Bardo Museum, Tunis.*

Islands of Madeira and the Canaries, and opening up several valuable new trade routes. Hamilco was another skilled seaman who turned his attention to the coasts of Gaul and Cornwall in search of tin; as a result of these activities the Carthaginians were now well and truly back into the import and export business. By the end of the fifth century, they had made a good recovery, but had made numerous enemies among their neighbours by their rampages throughout the Mediterranean.

Their main targets were Sardinia and the Greek cities of Sicily, who were also at loggerheads with each other and posed a threat to the few Phoenician colonies that were still on the island. The conflict that broke out in 409 BC dragged on for a hundred years and resulted in the destruction of all the Greek cities, including Agrigento and Selinunte. Only Syracuse managed to weather the storm, each side inflicting great atrocities during the hostilities. On one occasion the Carthaginians wiped out three hundred Greek prisoners of war and on another the Greeks massacred the entire population of Motya in retaliation. Twice hard-pressed Carthage sued for peace and paid heavy indemnities, and then went back to the fight. Previously, she had avoided fighting on her home territory and so had escaped material damage to her cities in North Africa; moreover, most of the fighting had been done by mercenaries, and so they sustained the majority of the casualties.

Carthage had also amassed a great deal of loot from her victories, but in 310 BC the picture changed. Agathocles, the Tyrant of Syracuse, sailed to Cap Bon with fourteen thousand men and took the war to the very doorstep of Carthage. Remaining in North Africa for three years, he raided the Carthaginian estates and kept in touch with Sicily by fleets of vessels, which he built with Greek aid in the ports of Utica and Bizerta.

In an effort to prevent a national disaster, the Carthaginians turned again to their deities, Baal and Tanit, whom they felt they had in some way grievously offended. They proceeded to sacrifice five hundred children, including infants up to the age of three years, mostly the first-born of the leading families. In less serious crises, the children of slaves were often substituted, but on this occasion there were no alternatives. The sacrifices took place at night. The victims were ceremoniously strangled in public before being burnt in the fires of Baal. Their ashes were placed in urns and interred with prayers of consecration (*Ill. 5*). For the Carthaginians, the sacrifices worked. The gods were appeased and Agathocles returned to Sicily without provoking a major confrontation. They heaved a sigh of relief, paid an indemnity, and kept as slaves their Greek prisoners of war, who were to influence their future standard of living.

During the next fifty years or so before the start of the First Punic War, Carthage absorbed a great deal of Greek culture. The standard of living rose, the luxuries of life were in great demand and appreciated. Plumbing was introduced to the villas of the wealthy. Jewellery, perfumes and chic Greek clothing were used to excess by fashionable women, as can be seen from the cosmetic boxes and the collections of jewellery that have been found and are now in the Bardo Museum. The men, on the other hand, were more staid and did not alter their way of life. They still kept their beards and wore the skull cap and robes of their forebears (*Ill. 6*), loose

5 *Rows of Punic stele marking the graves of sacrificed infants in the Tophet sanctuary of Baal, Carthage.*

6 *Funerary stele of a Carthaginian, from Maktar. His robe is very similar to the jellaba still worn in Tunisia, and the skull cap is also a common piece of headgear there.*

garments possibly not unlike the jellaba worn by many in Morocco and Tunisia today. Plutarch found little to commend in them, calling them 'a hard and gloomy race, obstinate, austere, and with little taste for frivolity', and also accused them of being lecherous and obsequious to their superiors.

Education now included Greek and not a few students went on to the University of Athens, where one named Clitomachus eventually had the honour of being elected Chancellor. Fraternisation with the Greeks progressed to the point of intermarriage. Hannibal himself was half Greek and the sons of the hierarchy of the local African tribes often took local Carthaginian girls as wives. They adopted Punic customs, giving their children Punic names, and some went so far as to adopt the Punic gods. The Carthaginians themselves set up shrines to the goddesses Persephone and Demeter in the hope that they would look favourably on their agricultural activities. The tribes too were organising themselves into separate kingdoms. Mauretania under the Moors became a separate state and the two powerful Numidian tribes in Algeria, the Masaesyli and the Massyli, centred themselves on Siga and Cirta respectively; the Massyli being nearest to the Carthaginians' western border. The tribes beyond the mountains and in the deserts such as the Gaetules, the Nasamones and, of course, the Garamantes, remained unaffected and carried on with their lucrative caravan trade from Senegal and other parts of the interior.

The Greeks of Syracuse were harassing the Italian colonists, who appealed not only to Rome but also to the Carthaginians for aid. The Romans feared that this would give the Carthaginians an excuse to take over the island, and the Carthaginians likewise feared that Rome would do so, thus creating a situation that was to provoke the First Punic War in 264 BC.

The Romans realised that they could not dislodge the Carthaginians without destroying their sea power and to this end they built a fleet of a hundred quinqueremes based on the design of a Carthaginian vessel that had come into their possession. They added spiked grappling irons called crows to their vessels, to assist in boarding the enemy at close quarters, but in spite of all their efforts the force was inadequate and not very successful. By 528 BC, they had put together a much bigger fleet to transport an army commanded by Regulus to North Africa. However, in spite of some early gains, this expedition also failed for in 525 BC they lost some 17,000 men in a decisive battle with the Carthaginians led by Xanthippus of Sparta, to whom they had turned for assistance. The return journey with the few Carthaginian ships they had managed to capture was also a disaster. Thousands more lost their lives when the remainder of the force foundered on the rocks in a fierce gale before making harbour. In spite of this setback they built a third and larger fleet and of this new navy they lost another 150 ships in more fierce storms. By now the casualty list numbered some 100,000 men, and they had depleted their resources almost to the limit of the Treasury.

On the other hand Hamilcar Barka, the father of Hannibal, had done well with his mercenary armies in Sicily and, in view of the Roman losses, setbacks and misfortunes, they became increasingly negligent. To save money as well as to reduce the cost of keeping men at arms, they laid up their fleet. Nevertheless the Romans quietly persisted, and in 243 BC, having built a fourth and bigger fleet of 200 quinqueremes, set sail again, and took the Carthaginians unawares, this time conclusively winning the day at the battle of the Aegates Islands. Carthage lost Sicily and the islands for ever and over the next ten years had to pay Rome a huge indemnity.

This, however, was not the end of her troubles. On returning to Carthage from Sicily, the mercenaries of Hamilcar did not receive their due pay. Carthage, having in mind the expenses they had incurred and the sums due to Rome, pleaded poverty and dispatched the mercenaries with a small pittance to far-off Le Kef in Tunisia, where they hoped they would be 'out of sight and out of mind'. But the mercenaries, at last realising that no more funds were forthcoming, rose in a body and marched on Carthage. The Carthaginians, now in a panic, were prepared to pay up, but it was too late to prevent another disaster. This was the beginning of a bitter conflict described by Polybius as the 'Mercenary War'. The mercenaries were further encouraged by two hot-heads, the slaves Spendius and Matho, who stirred up and conscripted those Africans around Carthage who had been heavily suppressed and forced to contribute handsomely to the Sicilian campaigns.

The war was to last three years and once again extreme cruelty was indulged in on both sides. The mercenaries badly mutilated their prisoners of war by removing all their appendages before burying them alive; whilst Hamilcar, for the Carthaginians, trampled his victims under the feet of his elephants. Each side endeavoured to outdo the other in its cruelty. Spendius himself led a party to seek a truce, and they were all promptly crucified. The war ended only when the tribes of the Masaesyli on the western borders of Carthage joined with the Carthaginians to settle the issue. The final confrontation is said to have taken place in the Valley of the Axes, which is on the road to Bou Fica near Zaghouan.

In the meantime, Rome, taking advantage of the war in North Africa, had seized Sardinia; they then demanded another large indemnity from the Carthaginians, who could do little else but pay up again. In order to find these large sums demanded by Rome, and with a depleted treasury, Carthage had to look elsewhere for cash. Spain, with her ample resources of silver, tin and copper, was the obvious answer. Hamilcar, with his son-in-law Hasdrubal, and Hannibal, then a boy of nine who, Livy records, begged not to be left behind, went to Spain and eventually conquered the whole of the south. On the death of Hamilcar, Hasdrubal consolidated the position over the next sixteen years, founded a new capital called Cartagena or New Carthage, struck coins and married a Spanish wife, his first wife having died. On Hasdrubal's death in 215 BC, Hannibal found himself Head of State at the age of twenty and, three years later, in 212 BC he made his epic journey over the Alps into Italy with his elephants. It was the first time the Romans had seen the creatures and for the next seventeen years Hannibal was the scourge of the country, winning all the encounters and taking the war to the gates of Rome itself. Of all the defeats suffered by the Romans during this period, the worst was the battle of Cannae in 216 BC where few survived. Amongst those who did was the younger Scipio, who eventually brought about Hannibal's final defeat.

After Cannae, the Senate sent Scipio to Spain with a large force to cut Hannibal's lines of communication. In this they were so successful that they not only took Cartagena but eventually managed to clear the remainder of the Carthaginians out of the peninsula. Hannibal had now lost his capital and his base, and was isolated in Italy. Hasdrubal, who had left Spain for lack of help and reinforcements from Carthage and under pressure from Scipio's successful legions, arrived in Italy to join Hannibal and give him what help he could. However, before he could reach his brother, he was defeated and killed at the battle of the River Metaurus, and his head was delivered to Hannibal at his camp in southern Italy.

In spite of Scipio's achievements in Spain and the fact that he returned to Rome a hero, the Senate refused to grant him a Triumph on the bureaucratic grounds that he was not of consular rank. He therefore held his own celebrations, putting on show the six hundred tons of silver and loot that he had brought back with him and sacrificing one hundred oxen on the altars of the temple of Jupiter Capitolinus. He was thirty years old, tall, wore his hair long, and dressed like a Greek. After a great deal of argument with the Senate, Scipio finally persuaded them to let him carry the war to North Africa, realising that this could very possibly draw Hannibal out of Italy. The historian Coelius, writes of his departure in 204 BC: 'there were so many men in his force that when they shouted the birds of the air fell dead at the sound'.

The political intrigues that developed amongst the Cathaginians and the Numidians after Scipio had left Italy were so intricate that they could well be the scenario for a tragic opera, and the sequence of events is complicated.

Before leaving Italy, Scipio had made an alliance with Syphax, the king of the Numidian tribe of the Masaesyli, but before Scipio could reach North Africa, Syphax, who was now an old man, had met Sophonisba, the very young and beautiful daughter of the general in command of the defence of Carthage, whom Scipio had recently thrown out of Spain. According to Livy, he at once married her and switched his allegiance to Carthage, Scipio then enlisted the aid of Masinissa, the king of the other Numidian tribe which was based in Utica; the Carthaginians, to combat this threat, set Syphax against Masinissa. They had never been friendly but, unfortunately, in the fracas that ensued, Masinissa and his following had the worst of the battle and he fled to southern Tunisia to drum up more support.

By now Scipio had landed and after a few preliminary skirmishes, he discovered the positions of the Carthaginian troops and the Numidian camps of Syphax. Under cover of darkness he set them alight, routed their combined armies and went on to take Tunis. In view of this turn of events Masinissa hurried back from southern Tunisia and captured Cirta where Syphax had his palace, with Sophonisba still in residence. According to Livy again, as soon as he saw her he too fell in love with her and married her the same day. The Numidians were not ones to let the grass grow under their feet. Scipio was furious. He had planned to exhibit Sophonisba in Rome and told Masinissa in no uncertain terms that she was not his property but was a prisoner of the Roman Senate. Masinissa accepted the situation with bad grace, but not wishing to see Sophonisba suffer the humiliation of a Roman spectacle sent her a cup of poison, which it is recorded that she drank saying, 'I accept this bridal gift'.

As Scipio had forseen, Hannibal left Italy, and on 25 October 202 BC his legions, supported by the troops of Masinissa, met the Carthaginians at the battle of Zama. It marked the end of the Second Punic War – the defeat of Hannibal was one of the most significant in the history of Rome. Had Rome lost, it would have been a Carthaginian culture that predominated throughout the Mediterranean and this could have had a widespread influence in the later centuries.

Zama is the Jama of today, quite near to Siliana, and it is difficult to realise that the open country here was once the site of a turning point in history. Scipio returned to Rome whilst still in his early thirties, this time to a legitimate Triumph. Livy declared it to be the 'Triumph Omnium Clarrissimus', the finest ever. Appian, in his writings of AD 105, describes the procession: 'The trumpets, the spoils, the gold and the silver bullion, the crowns presented to him by the grateful cities, the music of the harpists and the flute players, the elephants, and the oxen for the sacrifice, and of course the Carthaginian nobles as prisoners of war with Syphax in chains'. It was a spectacle that Sophonisba had avoided; as a final accolade Scipio was given the title of Africanus by the Senate.

Carthage was divested of her colonies, her navy and her elephants, and all the wealth she had derived from Sicily. The limit of her boundaries was marked by a trench dug from Tabarca to Sfax, the rest of the territory being given to Masinissa. As a final blow Carthage had to find an indemnity to Rome amounting to a thousand talents.

Hannibal fled and in 195 BC sought refuge with the King of Bithynia at Nicomedia in Asia Minor, today's Ismir near Istanbul where, after twelve years, he became a political liability and committed suicide. His tomb is still pointed out there. Masinissa was also awarded a Triumph in Rome, the first African to gain such an honour, and was appointed by the Senate to be the King of Numidia. He lived on for many years and had the wit and the talent to convert a tribal community into a kingdom which was developed into a complex of numerous agricultural estates.

Masinissa, like most Numidians, was devious and wily. He gradually extended his borders by quietly taking over the outlying and more vulnerable of the Carthaginian farms, knowing that they could not retaliate wih force. After her defeat, Rome had banned Carthage from taking part in any degree of armed conflict and her protests to Rome about the activities of Masinissa went unheeded. Once more Carthage had become a wealthy nation due to the merchants' trading acumen and they were again conspicuous in the cities of the eastern Mediterranean. Cato in 153 BC was so amazed at their standard of agriculture compared to the poor showing of the farmers in Italy that on his return from North Africa, and to prove his point, he nonchalantly produced in the Senate some large and luscious figs which he had brought back with him, stating that Africa was merely three days' sailing from Ostia with a favourable wind.

In 154 BC, Masinissa finally overreached himself when he annexed the town of Souk El Khemis, together with the surrounding country. For the Carthaginians it was the final straw and they retaliated with force, a conflict that Masinissa won at the age of eighty–eight. Rome suddenly realised that the Cathaginians were well on the way to becoming a powerful faction, in spite of their previous severe defeat, and considered their retaliation an excuse to intervene. They also thought that Masinissa, if left to his own devices, could also pose a threat by becoming too powerful. Thus the Third Punic War began in 149 BC when the Roman legions landed at Utica.

The Carthaginians found on negotiation that the terms of surrender demanded by Rome were so unacceptable that they had no option but to fight to the end, a period of three years of misery and privation. They put up an heroic but hopeless fight for, regardless of all their efforts, Carthage fell in 146 BC. It was the result of a final assault led by Scipio Aemelianus, the grandson of Africanus. Appians' account reads like the fall of Jerusalem in AD 72. It was a blood bath. Over a period of ten days or so the Carthaginians were slowly pushed from the lower town back up the Byrsa hill, through the narrow streets with their blocks of six-storey houses on either side. The cruelty was unbelievably vicious. The houses were taken one by one, the inhabitants being forced to the upper rooms, thence to the roof tops to be flung down from there and the windows into the alleys and gutters below. Planks were put from one roof to another and those hurled to the streets were trodden down by the excited horses of the Roman advance, even before the bodies could be cleared away into the pits that had been dug for them. Strabo estimates that the City held 700,00 at the beginning of the siege and of those only 50,000 remained alive at the end. Many escaped, as others had done before the siege, to seek refuge in Maktar. Here they set up a colony in what was then a Numidian town, their descendants remaining there for many generations.

The siege ended when Hasdrubal, the commander of the defence, surrendered with the last of his men in the Temple of Eshmoun on the summit of the Byrsa Hill; but his wife and children, overcome with disgust at his cowardly decision, walked down into the City fires. Punic Carthage was razed and Scipio had the site cursed and strewn with salt. The territories once held by the Carthaginians were incorporated into a new order known as *Provincia Africa*, and Utica became the capital with a Roman Governor to administer the Province. Nothing really tangible remains of Punic Carthage apart from the Punic ports and the very sad Tophet sanctuary tucked away amongst the houses of a modern suburb.

In Punic times the Tophet sanctuary extended over a much greater area than it does today, but here amongst the remains that have come to light one can see the crematorium where once burnt the fires of Baal. The various headstones of the different periods that marked the burials stand in serried ranks (*Ill. 5*). In a garden shed, stacked in rows, there are many of the stelae, each with the sign of the goddess Tanit, a solar disc on an upturned crescent moon, and all inscribed with the ritual dedications. On a shelf are some of the pottery urns which once held the ashes; when the contents of these were sifted they produced the teeth of infants up to three years of age. There is one unique stela in the Bardo Museum which has engraved on it not the insignia of Tanit, but the figure of a priest carrying a very small infant in the crook of his arm to the sacrifice. This one object more than any other underlines a horrific religious conviction that had its origins far back in the cults of the ancient Middle East.

Carthage (*Ill. 50*) was protected by a wall twenty-one miles long, and this had in its construction a series of towers and barracks with stabling for 4000 horses and 300 elephants in walls that were eight metres thick. The Agora was near the port and from here the streets and houses went up to the summit of the Hill of Byrsa; interestingly enough it is in this area where quantities of ashes have been found in the soil. The Punic ports had two basins, one for the merchant vessels and one for the naval fleet, both basins being interconnected by a canal. On an island located in the naval basin were the buildings that housed those who controlled the shipping. There were dry dock facilities for 220 vessels and, according to Polybius who was present at the destruction of Carthage, a series of Ionic columns marked the entrance to the harbours. Recent excavations have confirmed much of the ancient authors' descriptions. The ship sheds provided the base measurements for a full size reconstruction of a trireme built in the shipyards of the Piraeus and successfully launched in July 1987. It is a properly commissioned ship in the Greek navy.

The cities that were founded by the Romans as a result of their increasing occupation of Africa after the fall of Carthage were very often developed on the sites of the old Punic towns. Having to adapt to the sites meant that, in many cases, they could not follow closely the principles of Hippodamus of Miletus, the 'father' of town planning on the grid system. This is very typical of some of the wheat towns such as Dougga, the ancient Thugga in Tunisia. Hippodamus' grid principle had a main street, the Decumanus Maximus, and often a secondary intersecting street, the Cardo Maximus, joined by a series of connecting streets. These divided the town into more or less equal blocks or 'insulae'. These blocks were either shops or houses, or sometimes the large villas of the wealthy which faced onto the street. The military towns built by the Third Augustan Legion, such as Timgad, are good examples of this town planning and were built with precision.

The municipal buildings and the temples were often around the Forum, which was the hub of the town and part of the Civic Centre. Here stood the Capitol and the temple dedicated to the town's patron deity, also the Civic Basilica which housed the law courts and the town's administration. Around the Forum there were often shops under colonnades. There were markets for food and sometimes a cloth market, often built by a wealthy citizen and donated to the town. The public baths were usually built in different sectors of the town, it being the common practice to have more than one of these establishments. Here were the public latrines and, more often than not, there was situated, very conveniently next to the principal baths, the 'House of Ill Repute'. Everyone went to the baths where they spent a great deal of their leisure hours discussing the topics of the day and the scandals that were rife in any Roman city.

The theatres were usually built into the side of a hill to give the auditorium elevation over the stage and the *scaena frons*, which was the permanent backdrop to the stage. The sites were carefully chosen and were built wherever possible to command the finest views over the countryside. Sometimes there was a smaller theatre or odeon that was used for concerts or for meetings of the Town Council. The large hippodromes and the amphitheatres were built outside the town centres, or in some nearby locality with a flat terrain.

During the later centuries wealthy citizens often built and donated to the town libraries and other municipal amenities. In the first and second centuries AD the entrances to towns and cities were embellished with fine Triumphal Arches that were dedicated by the citizens to the Emperor they wished to honour. There are possibly more of these arches in North Africa than anywhere else in the Empire. An abundance of marble was used in the civic buildings which included a host of columns in different coloured stone. Lavish mosaic floors were laid in the wealthy villas and these were often made in special workshops and put down in sections. The marble came from Italy and other sources in the Empire, but the red marble that was so popular with Hadrian was quarried at Simitthus, the modern Chemtou in Tunisia.

3

Cyrene and Cyrenaica

The Phoenicians had not found the country and the rugged coasts of Cyrenaica suitable for their early trading ports in the Mediterranean, preferring those further to the west, but for the Greeks it was ideal. The City States on the Greek mainland and islands were becoming very overpopulated and, in the seventh century BC, the situation was made a good deal worse by the effects of a prolonged drought.

Herodotus relates how the first emigrant Greeks to leave for North Africa came from the island of Thera (Santorini), north of Crete. The fertile lands and the climate of Cyrenaica were very similar to those of Greece itself, and this was one of the main attractions. The waters around the island of Platea, just off the coast, had for a long time past been fished for sponges and it was here that the first Greeks settled. One adult male was chosen by lot from each family and the lucky (or unlucky) ones left home for Platea, hardly relishing, no doubt, the prospect of the unknown hardships which they might have to face.

After two years, the colony moved to Aziris, just opposite on the mainland, and evidence of their arrival on this barren and exposed site is attested by potsherds and other artefacts. By 630 BC, they had become more or less integrated with the local tribes, with whom they intermarried, and Cyrene was founded by their leader Battus on the upper slopes of a hill which gave onto a high plateau. From this hill there were – and still are – extensive and uninterrupted views over the lower reaches of fertile land which extended to the sea. Once they were established on this site, they were joined by more colonists from the Peloponese and many of the other Greek islands. Further colonies sprang up along the coast which had their origins in early fishing expeditions; a few of these eventually developed into the cities of Ptolemais, Derna, Euhesperides (Benghazi) and Apollonia, which in due course became the busy and important port for nearby Cyrene. Little remains of Apollonia today, a few columns and the foundations of the harbour stretching out into the clear blue sea. Local legend has it that the town was a favourite resort of Cleopatra when she wished to escape from the rigours of life in Alexandria. However, Apollonia, fine town though it was, could not in any way have compared with the luxuries and the sophistication of Alexandria; but it was the next coastal town of note west of Alexandria and so the legend may indeed be true.

During the latter part of the sixth century BC Cyrene minted coinage. On the obverse ('heads') was usually the head of Zeus Ammon with the curved horns of a ram coming from his brow; and on the reverse was a representation of the silphium plant. This appears to have been a cross between a leek and an onion, judging from the coins (*Ill. 7*), and was indigenous to Cyrenaica. It formed a major export to Greece and Rome, for it was impossible to grow it elsewhere. The roots could be pickled, the leaves eaten as a vegetable and the sap used as a flavouring agent. It was also valued for its medicinal properties, but it did have one great drawback, it stank to high heaven. Its name in the vernacular was *asafoetida*, which descriptively translates as 'Devil's dung'. The Greeks and the Romans had a palate for pungent flavours, but unfortunately, and this no doubt was due to overharvesting, the plant became extinct sometime during the first century AD.

7 *Silver didrachm of Cyrene of the late fourth century BC. On the obverse is the head of Zeus Ammon wearing the ram's horn which was his attribute; on the reverse is a fine example of the siliphium plant, now extinct in the area. A major temple to the god was located in the Oasis of Siwa.*

Silphium was not Cyrene's only export. Fine horses were reared on the plateau, as well as corn, fruit and, of all things, roses. Theophrastus, the father of botany and a pupil of Plato and Aristotle, describes the variety grown there as 'five-petalled either red or white'; according to his researches the sweetest scented varieties came from Cyrene. They were propagated by cuttings and made the best distilled perfumes. Pliny, Virgil, Cicero and Juvenal all refer to them in their writings.

Roses were used for garlands and in bouquets at most of the Roman festivals, and were sold by the flower girls on the street corners in Rome. Suetonius states that Nerva, who built the Way of Nerva from Tangiers to Alexandria in AD 98, spent four million sesterces just to decorate one of his banquets with them. Cleopatra, adopting the Roman custom, used them for many official functions and garlands of them have been found in Romano-Egyptian tombs from the second to fourth centuries AD. Not only were roses emblems of love associated with Cupid, they also represented the god of silence. Confidences disclosed at a banquet by those wearing such a wreath were committed to silence and they were in fact 'sub rosa'. The custom passed into the early Christian church but did not become popular, for it brought to mind Roman debauchery. However, in spite of this, they were still used in Christian ritual throughout the Middle Ages and particularly in the ninth century, when great quantities were grown in the monastery gardens in England, notably in Winchester. On certain occasions they were also worn as crowns by the priests of St Paul's.

In the sixth century BC, disputes arose between the Greeks of Cyrene and the local Berber tribes, which could have included the Nasamones who habitually left their cattle to graze by the coast in the summer whilst they went to gather dates from the Oasis of Jalo, 130 miles inland. A fine bronze Berber head, now in the British Museum, was found in the ruins of the Temple of Zeus Ammon and could well illustrate this tribe.

The Greeks were by now very prosperous, a state of affairs that had caused the Libyans to regard themselves as an unwanted second-class population, and the fermenting enmity erupted in 570 BC into a serious fracas. The Libyans enlisted the help of the Egyptians and attacked the Greeks, who were hard put to keep control and subdue the revolt. During the reign of Trajan another much more serious revolt, which almost developed into a state of civil war, came about in AD 115 and involved the then large Jewish community in Cyrene. The great damage inflicted by the rioting in the city was very extensive and included the destruction of the Temple of Apollo. It was so widespread, in fact, that restoration and recovery would have been quite impossible without the generous aid granted by Hadrian. Simon of Cyrene, who was co-opted by the Roman soldiers in Jerusalem to carry the Cross to Golgotha, must have previously been one of this populace.

In 528 BC, Cyrenaica became a part of the Persian Empire, being taken over after the Persians had invaded and conquered Egypt. The Persian Satraps in Alexandria showed very little interest in their territories west of Tobruk, so that life in Cyrene and the associated cities was not altered or disrupted in any way. The inhabitants became even more prosperous than they had been, their affluence being reflected in the fine tombs and the architecture of this period. Roman influence in the country progressed even more after the fall of Alexandria to Julius Caesar in 47 BC. Cyrene had become a Roman province in 74 BC, but the inhabitants of the cities for the most part remained Greek-speaking and orientated to Greek culture in spite of the Roman administration.

Two references are particularly important in casting light on life here during the late first century BC. One is a letter from Agrippa to Cyrene and mentioned by Josephus. It states: 'On behalf of the Jews of Cyrene, Augustus has already written to the praetor of Libya, Florius, and to the other officials of the Province that the sacred monies should be sent to Jerusalem in accordance with their ancestral custom without hindrance. They have now come before me to complain that they are being threatened by certain informers and prevented from sending the money on the pretext of tax payments which are not due. I order that restoration be made to them, that they be in no way molested and that, in whatever cities the sacred money has been taken, those charged with these matters restore that money to the Jews there'.

The other is a very long edict of Augustus, from about 7 or 6 BC and it is the first part that is of interest:

'Imperator Caesar Augustus, pontifex maximus, in his 17th year of tribunician power, imperator 14 times, proclaims: Since I find that there are in total 215 Romans of every age in the province of Cyrene who have a census rating of 2500 denarii or more, from which number jurors are drawn, and that within this number exist certain cliques; and since embassies from the cities of the province have complained that these cliques have acted oppressively against the Greeks on capital charges, when the same people take it in turns to act as prosecutors and witnesses; and since I have myself learnt that innocent individuals have been oppressed in this way and have been consigned to the ultimate penalty, it is my view that, until the Senate deliberates on this matter or I myself come up with something better, the governors of the province of Crete and Cyrenaica will act well and properly if they appoint the same members of Greek jurors from the highest census groups in the province of Cyrene as of Romans, none being younger than 25, whether Greek or Roman and none having a census rating and property of less than 7500 denarii, or if on this system the number of jurors needed cannot be obtained, let them appoint as jurors in capital cases men with half – and not less than half – this census rating. If a Greek is on trial, being permitted the right, on the day before the accuser begins his statement to decide whether he wants the jury to be Roman or half Greek, and chooses that half the jurors be Greek, the balls are to be apportioned and inscribed with names. The names of the Romans are to be drawn from one urn, the names of the Greeks from the other, until 25 of each race have been selected'–

and so on. Life in those days was basically not so very different from now.

In AD 98, Nerva built and extended the coast road which ran from Tangiers to Leptis in Tripolitania, through Cyrenaica to Tobruk and the Egyptian border, linking the coastal cities including Apollonia on the way. Legend records that the border separating Libya from Cyrenaica was fixed by two brothers from Carthage, who ran from Leptis to meet two others sent from Cyrene, both envoys making a simultaneous start. The Greeks of Cyrene accused the Libyans of cheating and the two from Leptis, to demonstrate their innocence, demanded to be buried alive at the border. The road of Nerva now passes under the imposing Arch of the Philaeri, which was raised to commemorate their sacrifice. It was nostalgically dubbed by the troops of the Eighth Army in the Second World War, 'The Marble Arch'.

Cyrene was the most important and the most interesting of the cities of Cyrenaica. Built on a broad shelf just under the edge of the plateau, it was very reminiscent of Delphi in mainland Greece, with its back to the hills and with similar far-reaching views. Like Alexandria it was Hellenistic in its layout and conception. The main street of Battus, which traversed the city centre, led to his tomb in the Agora, where there were shops and a colonnade. At the north-west aspect and at the back of the Agora are the ruins of the gymnasium and on the south side are the remains of the Temple of Jupiter. The most impressive feature, however, is the Forum, enclosed by a wall and more imposing colonnades. The podium and the steps of the Caesarium are just off centre, whilst the Basilica takes up the whole length of the north-east side. The monumental gate to the area is in the south wall and opposite across the street of Battus is the Roman theatre, one of four in the city, with a few tiers of seats still *in situ*.

There is a little odeon situated immediately behind the north-west aspect of the Forum, but not now in a good state of repair. In addition to the Roman theatre near the Forum, another was built at a later date next to the market. The fourth was a large Greek theatre, which was also at a later date converted into a Roman amphitheatre; this was situated at the extreme north-west aspect of the city and built into the city wall. To the east of this theatre, not far from the Temple of Apollo, and built near to the city wall, are the large Baths of Trajan. The two sanctuaries of note were that of Apollo in the lower part of the city, situated near the sacred spring known as Apollo's Fountain, and another further to the north-east, dedicated to Zeus Ammon. The original Temple to Apollo was in the Doric order and completed in the middle of the sixth century BC, but was rebuilt at a later date after its destruction during the Jewish riots. The new temple was a much larger structure, 69 × 30 metres, also of the Doric order, and was completed at the end of the sixth century. Sufficient remains today to indicate its magnificent proportions, with a command-ing flight of stairs giving access to the interior. The site chosen for the temple was the only one possible to enhance its dignity and presence in context with the surrounding buildings. The temple was extremely wealthy and several inscriptions relating to it are still extant. One from the reign of Nero runs: 'To Iatrus and Iaso, for the victory and safety of Nero Claudius Caesar Augustus Drusus Germanicus imperator and his whole house, the priests of Apollo provided statues from the funds of Apollo in the priesthood of Tiberius Claudius Apollonius, son of Priscus'.

The Temple of Zeus was dedicated to the cult of Zeus Ammon, which was also related to the Oracle of Zeus in his temple at Siwa Oasis. It was this oracle that was consulted by Alexander the Great when he passed through Egypt on his way to Asia Minor. The cult statue in Cyrene of the Olympian Zeus was a venerated copy of the masterpiece of Pheidias, which he made in his workshop close to the sanctuary of the god in Olympia. Many other temples enriched the city; of these the most notable is that dedicated to Demeter, the patroness of agriculture. The Hippodrome was somewhat isolated, well away from the city precincts and east of the Temple of Zeus, and so too was the cathedral built during the Byzantine period.

Today one can walk through the open countryside from Cyrene to Apollonia on the coast, past numerous early Greek tombs which differ in size and design, often carved with an architectural façade. They litter the hillside, silent, empty and desolate, with dim interiors, lintels sprouting weeds from the cracks in the stone, and foundations obscured with tall grasses.

4

North Africa from Julius Caesar to Hadrian

The end of the Third Punic war, and the final destruction of Carthage in 146 BC, marked the beginning of a new era in North Africa. As a result of the three Punic Wars Rome had acquired Sicily and Sardinia, Corsica, Spain and, lastly, Africa, which was henceforth governed by a Senator who was appointed on a yearly basis. Sole authority for the administration, which included the judicial and the military, was vested in him; he was also responsible for the collection of the taxes, a function open to abuse so that many made fortunes.

Much of Carthage's agricultural land was sold off to rich absentee landlords and to those who had not taken part in the wars. Other peasant farmers from Italy were emigrating to the country and many Italian merchants were heading for Cirta and the other African ports, all in the search for a better life. At a later date the Gracchi brothers, to further their agricultural policies in Rome, endeavoured, but not very successfully, to persuade a great many more to leave Italy and settle in Tunisia. As it was, the production of wheat from those farms that had already been established was beginning by now to increase very rapidly.

In recompense for the help he had given Scipio in the Second Punic War Masinissa had been awarded a Triumph in Rome, and had also been made the client King of Numidia, but by this time he had died at the age of eighty-eight, just before Scipio Minor, the grandson of Africanus, razed Carthage to the ground. Micipsa, whose two brothers had also died, succeeded him, and remained loyal to Rome. But of these two brothers, one had a bastard son Jugurtha, who lived up to his birthright. Jugurtha was older than Hiempsal and Adherbal, the two natural sons of Micipsa and, in order to get him out of the way, he was sent to Spain in 134 BC to command the Numidian cavalry, who were to assist Scipio in putting down a rebellion that had developed in the south. His relations all fervently hoped that he would not come back, but he was a competent soldier who was very popular with the troops, and managed to conduct himself so well that Scipio sent him back at the end of hostilities with a glowing report and a commendation.

Shortly after Jugurtha's return Micipsa died, leaving all the three young men joint heirs to the Kingdom, a situation that was obviously quite impossible. Jugurtha seized the chance to gain sole control and murdered Hiempsal. Adherbal was defeated in the attempt to exact retribution for his brother's murder, and fled to Rome to plead his cause. Jugurtha followed him to bribe the influential friends that he had made in Spain whilst with Scipio, but the Senate finally awarded half the Kingdom to Adherbal. It was a judgement of Solomon, but they did not attempt to back up the ruling with any military aid.

Back in Numidia the situation between Jugurtha and Adherbal did not improve, and war again broke out between them. This ended in 112 BC with the murder of Adherbal. Jugurtha now made his cardinal mistake, precipitating what Sallust records as 'The Jugurthine War'. Before he was killed, Adherbal had had a great deal of support from the citizens of Cirta, so Jugurtha attacked the city, killing all the males of the population without quarter, including all those of Italian descent. Naturally, this could not be overlooked by Rome. The Senate at once sent out some legions under Marius and his junior commander Sulla but Jugurtha, who was a good tactitian, dragged the war on for six years. Towards the end of 105 BC, the legions of Marius made a forced march over the desert in an effort to confront Jugurtha in Gafsa, but finally it was the treachery of his father-in-law, King Bocchus of Mauretania who, having an eye on a large slice of Numidian territory, eventually double-crossed him and brought about his final defeat by handing him over in chains to Sulla. Jugurtha was taken to Rome and incarcerated in the prision under the Capitoline Hill, where he was eventually strangled, supposedly on the orders of Marius.

The Triumvirate in Rome consisting of Pompey, Crassus and Julius Caesar dates from 60 BC. It was Crassus who broke the main body of the slave revolt led by Spartacus in 70 BC, and he had become one of the richest men in Rome. His fortune had come from the estates of those wealthy citizens who had lost their lives under the proscriptions instituted by Sulla. By this means, Sulla could name those whom he considered were opposed to him, confiscate their property and cancel the civil rights of their descendants. After the formation of the coalition it was agreed that Caesar would command Gaul, Pompey would take Spain and Africa, and Crassus should have jurisdiction over Syria. As a result of this arrangement Crassus, who was not a healthy man, decided to go east with his legions to confront the Parthians, but before he left he entertained the whole of the Roman populace to a costly and magnificent banquet. It was the last that Rome was to see of him and his legions, for he lost his life and his men at the Battle of Carrhae, modern Harran in the vast wheat plains of eastern Anatolia. The whole expedition was a complete disaster for Rome. In order to arrange a truce with the Parthians, the ailing Crassus was lifted onto his horse to meet Surena, the commander of the Parthians; an encounter which ended in slaughter when Crassus was killed by Pomaxathres, a member of Surenas' staff.

In spite of Pompey's marriage to Julia, the daughter of Julius Caesar, he and Caesar were of different political opinions. It was the question of the consulship of 48 BC which led to the Civil War. Pompey aligned himself with the Senate against Caesar and persuaded them to pass a decree ordering Caesar to disband his legions before he sought re-election. Caesar requested Pompey to do likewise before he agreed, but Pompey refused. The decree was vetoed by the Tribunes who, for their action, were ejected from Rome, which gave them little option but to join Caesar in his camp. The Senate then declared Caesar to be a Public Enemy of the State and gave Pompey the task of protecting Italy, whereupon Caesar crossed the river Rubicon, the boundary, and the Civil Wars had begun.

Pompey's great advantage lay in the wealth of North Africa and the loyalty of his legions who were still there. He also had the support of the Numidian cavalry and the associated troops of Juba, the son of Hiempsal, who was now the King of Numidia. They had always been close friends and Juba heartily disliked Caesar. This dislike stemmed from an incident that had occurred some years before in Rome during the hearing of a law case in the Senate. Juba had criticised the clothing Caesar was wearing at the time and Caesar, in a fit of pique, had grabbed him by the beard and shaken his head vigorously. Juba also disliked Curio, another of Caesar's friends whom he had met in Rome, and it was Caesar's unfortunate choice to send Curio to North Africa with two legions to eliminate those who were still loyal to Pompey. As it turned out, it was one of the few major setbacks that Caesar suffered in the Civil Wars, for he lost not only Curio, but also the legions.

As Caesar advanced from Rome to the south of Italy the loyalty to Pompey of the citizens in many towns on the way faded dramatically. The armies of Pompey in Spain had already been defeated, but Caesar still suffered a humiliating defeat at Dyrrhachium, where Pompey forced him to retreat. However, Pompey lost the day on the plains of Pharsalus in Thessaly, in spite of his numerical supremacy. He escaped, eventually arriving in Alexandria, hoping to gain support from the legions that were still there. After the battle Caesar found in Pompey's tent in the empty camp an untouched meal, to which he helped himself, and in the tents of the other generals he came across great quantities of silver plate and goblets full of wine: a sign of their hasty departure. His dry comment when he surveyed the loot and the casualties on the field was that they had 'asked for it'.

Caesar learnt of Pompey's death when he reached Alexandria. The fact that it was Ptolemy XIII and the Egyptians who were responsible for Pompey's murder incensed Caesar, who had hoped to find him alive. He therefore fined Egypt roughly the equivalent of three million pounds and returned Pompey's body to be buried on his Italian estates.

Pompey's two sons had escaped from the battle at Pharsalus and so too did Metullus Scipio, Labienus, Petrieus, and Afranieus, all of them going on to North Africa where they were joined by Cato, who had marched with his legions from Cyrene along the coast road to Numidia to meet them. Between them they managed to raise ten legions, which had in addition the support of four units of the Numidian cavalry lent by Juba. Caesar was in no hurry to follow them, however. The charms of Cleopatra and Egypt occupied him for some months, a period marred only by the outbreak of a serious revolt against him, which he managed, with difficulty, to put down, before he returned to Rome to take the Civil War to North Africa.

Caesar left Marsala in Sicily on 28 December 47 BC with six legions and 2000 cavalry, but the fleet was split up by storms during the crossing and he landed at Sousse with just 3000 men of his contingent. After the landing, he moved east beyond Cap Bon to join up with the rest of the force that had come ashore at Leptis Minor, all of them going on to make camp at Ruspina, today's Monastir in Tunisia. By now they were short of food and the whole expedition faced disaster when a foraging party was surprised by a detachment of Numidian cavalry led by Labienus. It was a very difficult situation that Caesar managed to retrieve to his advantage. He had two valuable allies in North Africa, the Prince of Mauretania and a great friend of his called Sittius, who had recently fled from Rome in a hurry to escape his massive debts. Metullus Scipio, the father-in-law of Pompey, was persuaded by Cato to take supreme command of their forces, whilst he, Cato, remained in Utica with the headquarters. There was little action to begin with between the two sides apart from verbal abuse. Caesar declared that Scipio chose not to wear his purple cloak in the presence of Juba, and Scipio accused Caesar of the seduction of Eunoe, the wife of Prince Bogudes of Mauretania, which could well have been the truth, knowing Caesar's reputation in Rome.

To force the issue and provoke a confrontation Caesar moved to Thapsus where Scipio had a garrison and also kept the depot for the major concentration of their stores. Caesar, in order to enable him to intercept the greater part of these seaborne supplies, blockaded the town. The battle began on 6 April 46 BC. Juba had brought thirty elephants to the scene but, frightened by Caesar's javelins and his advancing men, they turned about, stampeded and trampled the forces of Scipio coming up behind. The shambles that followed caused the Numidian cavalry to take fright and they, also turning, caused even greater confusion and chaos so that, within a short space of time, Caesar was left the undisputed victor. His troops had by now got the bit between their teeth and were completely out of control. Out of the 50,000 troops Scipio had at the battle, 10,000 were killed before they had the chance to surrender. The few senators who were opposed to Caesar and had come to North Africa to support Scipio, confident in his success, also died. Scipio found himself cut off from the main body of his troops by the mercenaries of Sittius, and committed suicide. Cato, not wishing to fall alive into the hands of Caesar, did likewise. Africanus, who had once held the rank of consul in Rome, was captured, but his past glory did nothing to help his appeal for clemency and Caesar had him executed.

Juba and Petrieus, however, managed to get away unscathed from the battle and returned to Juba's capital where neither of them was accepted by the inhabitants, who threw them out. The populace had no wish to suffer any retribution Caesar might have had in mind, nor did they wish to be the unwilling participants in any grandiose scheme that Juba had for martyrdom. They had heard he intended to burn the city and perish in the flames. The two of them made a pact and, after a last meal together, they fought a duel. Petrieus was the first to die, followed by Juba, who was dispatched by a loyal slave. Sources seem to differ as to who was the first to die, some indicate that it is not known, but the fact remains that they both met their end, the sequence of the event being more or less academic.

Numidia was once more carved up, some of the territory going to the Prince of Mauretania, with land on the western borders going to Sittius to form a buffer state. The rest of the territory and the detachments of the famous cavalry were taken over by Rome, and a new province of *Africa Nova* formed and put under the governorship of Sallust; Caesar finally settling many of his veterans in the towns of El-Djem and Bizerta.

All Juba's personal possessions and the properties of those who had been loyal to Pompey were sold; those cities which had been involved with them were made to contribute an indemnity to Rome, not only in money, but also in wheat and olive oil. In this respect Leptis Magna came off very badly, because from her extensive groves she was one of the major sources of oil and had to contribute a vast quantity to fulfil her share.

At the time of Cato's suicide at the end of the Civil War in 43 BC, Utica was one of the important Punic ports. Cato himself was one of the senators who had gone to North Africa to support Scipio against Caesar and was a descendant of the elder Scipio, who had at one time uttered in a speech to the Senate the famous words 'Carthage must be destroyed'. In 308 BC, Agathocles occupied the city when he confronted Carthage and, in 144 BC, it became the capital of *Provinciae Africa* when it was made the first 'Free City', controlling in all a total area of 50,000 square miles. The most important feature left today at Utica is The House of the Fountain which demonstrates to some extent the standard of living at that time. Here one can see some variegated marble floors and others in mosaic with fishing motifs, and in the villa there are also the remains of lead plumbing. One wonders if the tin came from Cornwall as it did in the villas of Pompeii. The only other site of note, but not very picturesque, is the Punic necropolis, not a lot in all to evoke a mental picture of its turbulent past.

The end of the Civil War was not the end of the upheavals in North Africa. The veterans of Marius and Sulla had been given land for their retirement on the Numidian African borders, and Rome, having giving Bocchus the slice of western Numidia that he coveted, made Gauda, the half-wit brother of Jugurtha, king of the remainder. On his death, the state passed to his two sons, Hiempsal and Hierbas and these two, running true to form, also began fighting amongst themselves. One enlisted the aid of Sulla, who was now Dictator in Rome. The other wooed the followers of Marius who had recently died there, half mad, after a reign of terror characterised by the countless atrocities he had inflicted on the aristocracy.

At this juncture Sulla appointed the young Pompey to command the forces in North Africa. At the age of twenty-two, he had become Sulla's protégé, was a good horseman, adept at fencing, handsome, athletic and capable of great charm. However, he could also be arrogant and insufferable, for though he was a brilliant soldier, he was well aware of it. In due course he became one of Rome's most able generals – not only did he conquer Jerusalem, Judaea and Asia Minor, he also founded some thirty-nine cities and celebrated numerous Triumphs. He quickly defeated the Marians in 81 BC, Hierbas having lost his life in the battle which effectively left Numidia to Hiempsal. It is recorded that after the battle, Pompey spent some time in North Africa hunting elephants for relaxation before he returned to Rome. Back in Rome, he was given the title of 'Pompey the Great', but he did not consider the title sufficient reward for his efforts and promptly demanded a Triumph. Sulla gently pointed out that this honour was conferred only on those of the rank of senator or praetor but Pompey, in his brash arrogance, persisted to the point where Sulla, tired of the arguments, was finally worn down and agreed.

Before the end of 46 BC Caesar was back in Rome. Cleopatra, with her son Caesarion arrived there in the June of the following year. The Romans, full of curiosity, had turned out to see her spectacular entry, for in her retinue she had her Nubian slaves, her eunuchs and her court officials as she made her way to one of Caesar's villas on his estate in the Horti Transtiberina, now the Villa Pamphili. Possibly because of her opulence, the Romans generally took a hearty dislike to her, especially the matrons of the aristocracy, all of whom felt for Caesar's wife, Calpurnia. Cleopatra's airs and graces irritated them profoundly, the final indignity being the golden statue which Caesar had made of her in the likeness of Venus-Genetrix, and which he had set up in a prominent position in Rome.

Caesar was also at this time very preoccupied with the preparations for his four Triumphs: for Gaul, Pontus, Egypt and the last for North Africa. The young sister of Cleopatra, Arsinoe, was brought from Egypt to take part in the Egyptian Triumph. She had taken the side of her brother Ptolemy XIII in the revolt against Caesar in Egypt and was to walk behind the chariot in chains. Cleopatra considered that she should have died rather than face such a dishonourable situation. The young Juba, aged five, the son of the dead Juba of Numidia, was the show-piece of the African Triumph, for he too walked in chains behind the chariot, but at the end of the festivities he was taken into the household of Octavian, later the Emperor Augustus, to be brought up and educated as a Roman noble. It was one of Rome's best investments, for he turned out to be a very cultured individual and eventually became the Client King of Numidia.

The themes of the African Triumph were the luxuries from that province. Forty elephants and a giraffe took part in the procession. It was the first time that a giraffe had been seen in Rome and, apart from Juba, it

was the main attraction. Banners in poor taste, illustrating the deaths of Scipio and little Juba's father, were carried in front of the processions. In the evening when they had ended, a feast for 200,000 of the Roman people seated at 22,000 tables was prepared in the public squares throughout the city. This lasted well into the early hours of the morning, ending with a final procession lit by torches on the backs of the elephants for Caesar, as he was taken up the Via Sacra to his villa in a litter. The festivities went on for days. Other attractions were the lion-hunts – Sallust had shipped over forty of these animals from North Africa for the events. No less than four hundred elephants were included in the spectacles, and sea battles were arranged on artificial lakes especially constructed for the purpose. The numerous gladitorial contests staged were fought out bitterly to the death of one or other of the contestants. The vast expense of staging these celebrations was covered by the enormous wealth which Caesar had extracted from Egypt and North Africa. He watched it all with Cleopatra on his arm. Poor Calpurnia was not very much in evidence. Caesar's fifth and last Triumph celebrated his victories in Spain over the sons of Pompey, who had escaped from Thapsus in North Africa. Not long afterwards, at the age of 55, on the Ides of March, 44 BC, he was murdered.

8 Mosaic showing an African elephant being guided up a gangplank to board a ship, no doubt bound for the games in Rome. Late third century AD. Imperial Villa, Piazza Armerina, Sicily.

During the time of Hannibal and in the first and second centuries AD, elephants were very plentiful in the Maghreb, being quite possibly of a smaller species than those of Central Africa today. After their introduction into Italy by Hannibal they became more numerous and in later years were bred there and took part in most of the Triumphs of the Roman Emperors. They also figured in the games and the national festivals staged in the amphitheatres throughout Italy and North Africa, and they are depicted in some of the mosaic floors that are still *in situ* in Volubilis and on some that are now preserved in the Bardo Museum in Tunis. They also appear on some of the coinage of the period. In the mosaics in the Imperial Villa at Piazza Armerina in Sicily an elephant can be seen walking up the gangplank of a ship before being shipped from Africa (*Ill. 8*).

After Caesar's death his will, which had been given to the Vestal Virgins for safe keeping, was opened and read in the presence of his father-in-law, Lucius Piso, in the villa of Mark Antony in Rome. It left three-quarters of his estate, no mean sum, together with the name of Caesar to Octavian who was his adopted son and heir. At the time Octavian was with his friend Agrippa in Apollonia in Epirus – not the Apollonia in Cyrenaica – finishing his education and undergoing a course of military training as a junior officer with the legions at their headquarters. The Transtiberine Villa and gardens were left to the people of Rome, but Cleopatra and her son Caesarion were not mentioned in the will and, in the circumstances, Mark Antony advised them to return quietly to Egypt.

Mark Antony regarded Octavian as a somewhat despicable creature, not having a suitably noble background to fit him for high office. He maintained to all and sundry that his grandfather had originally come from North Africa, where he had kept a bakery and a scent shop, and in the Senate he endeavoured to prevent the terms of the will being carried out. Antony had, in point of fact, completely underestimated Octavian who, in spite of his untidy appearance, had a sharp mind and a strong will and returned at once from Apollonia to claim his inheritance. In this he was supported by the good will of the Senate, Cicero, and many other influential factions in Rome. This forced Mark Antony to a compromise and a Triumvirate was formed between the two of them and Lepidus. It was a period of great upheaval in Rome, for the proscriptions which had first been instituted by Sulla began again. Once more many senators and members of nobility lost their estates and their lives, including Cicero, who was apprehended and beheaded in his litter whilst endeavouring to escape from the City.

In spite of Mark Antony's dislike of Octavian, he did marry his sister Octavia, but this in no way hindered his future liaison with Cleopatra in the east. She had made a state visit to Tarsus, where he was at the time, in order to obtain his support against Octavian whom she accused of usurping the succession which, she considered, should have gone to Caesarion. Mark Antony became more and more besotted with Cleopatra, to the extent that he gave her the famous library in Pergamum and then for a time lived a life with her in Alexandria which was one round of pleasure, wearing exotic clothing and attending endless banquets. As a result of all this his relations with Octavian grew steadily worse. To force the issue Octavian, having just cleared the last troublesome adherents of Pompey out of Sicily, obtained Mark Antony's will from the Vestal Virgins and read it out to a meeting of the Senate. Mark Antony had not long before staged a splendid Triumph in Alexandria, which had angered the Senate. They were amazed to learn from the will that he had declared Caesarion his successor and that he had also left his estates to his two children by Cleopatra, the twins Alexander Helios and Cleopatra Selene. The Eastern Empire, he stated, was to go to Egypt according to the treaty he had recently signed in Antioch. The Senate acted quickly. It stripped him of his consulship and declared war on Egypt.

After losing the decisive battle of Actium in September 31 BC to Octavian, Antony and Cleopatra returned to Alexandria to be followed the next year by Octavian, who brought his legions through Syria to Egypt. He had also sent Cornelius Gallus to North Africa to bring the legions there to Alexandria via Cyrenaica. When he entered the city, he found Mark Antony dead, his troops and navy having defected to Octavian before his eyes. The death of Cleopatra followed on 30 August 30 BC, thus ending the two-and-a-half thousand years of rule by the Pharaohs. To celebrate the event Horace wrote an ode *Nunc est bibendum* (Now is the time to drink), and a commemorative series of coins were also struck bearing a crocodile and the legend 'Aegypto Capta'. It is considered that the holiday now kept by Rome on 15 August, though today a Church festival is, in reality, the anniversary of her death.

In Rome, Octavian held his Egyptian Triumph and Alexander Helios and Cleopatra Selene, both aged eight, and in chains, walked behind his chariot. Then, they too were brought up as Roman citizens in the household of Octavia, like the little Juba of Numidia.

Between the dates of the death of Caesar in Rome and the death of Cleopatra in Alexandria, the provinces of North Africa had passed from Octavian to Mark Antony and then to Lepidus. After the battle of Actium in 31 BC, Alexandria and the provinces came under the control of Rome, and after the conquest of Egypt Octavian found that he had almost 300,000 veterans in the legions. He has described in the *Res Gestae*, inscribed on his tomb, how he followed the precedent set by Caesar and settled vast numbers in North Africa at Le Kef and Thuburbo Maius. Many Italians were dispossessed of their land which was handed over to the veterans who had returned to Italy, and not a few returned to their home towns; many of those who had lost everything went to Africa to start afresh. Apart from these immigrants and the veterans, many wealthy Romans also invested in North African properties, becoming absentee landlords. One Rubellius Blandus, who was a friend of Augustus (Octavian had been given this title by the Senate in 27 BC), invested large sums, both in Africa and in Asia Minor.

To protect the well-being and the interests of those who had gone out to the new towns and settlements, Augustus raised the Third Augustan Legion. This was to police the country, for the new prosperity had brought an increase in raids and other incidents from the indigenous Berber tribes in the hills. It was largely due to the efforts of the legion that North Africa was able to develop its potential and become the great asset that it was to Rome.

In 27 BC, Augustus handed over the government of North Africa to the Senate. He considered that in view of the wealth it contributed to Rome in ivory, grain, wild beasts for the amphitheatres and olive oil, which one Senator in a complaint said, 'Smelt quite dreadful and did not match up in quality to the oil that was produced in Italy', it was politic for him not to be involved in the administration.

The Senate appointed as its agent a proconsul, to be resident in Carthage, who was also to be responsible for the over all command of the Third Augustan Legion, which was at that time established at Haidra. Two years later, in 25 BC, Juba II (*Ill. 9*), who as a child of five had walked in chains in Caesar's Triumph, now twenty-six years old, married Cleopatra Selene, the daughter of Antony and Cleopatra. She too had been brought up in the household of Octavia, the sister of Augustus, after taking part in his Triumph. King Bocchus of Mauretania had recently died, so in 25 BC, Augustus appointed Juba to be the Client King. He took over the old Capital of Bocchus and to honour Augustus he renamed the city 'Iol Caesarea', modern Cherchel. He built a theatre, a library and all the classical buildings that were to be found in a Roman capital. Apart from being a competent historian, Juba was also a discriminating connoisseur of art, especially of marble sculpture, and was responsible for collecting most of the treasures of the time that can be seen in the Cherchel museum today. There is also a magnificent collection of bronzes at Rabat in Morocco, which came from Volubilis, a city he founded as a second capital in what was then Mauretania. Another hoard of bronzes which are now in the Bardo Museum, Tunis, were recovered from a shipwreck in the bay of Tunis, and these are now thought to have been destined for his collections and not, as originally suggested, for Rome.

Though of Numidian descent, Juba's vast territory was still subject to raids from the hill tribes, which the legion helped him to restrain, for his loyalty to Rome was never in question. An interesting extant inscription dedicated to him reads, 'To King Juba, grandson of King Hiempsal, great-grandson of King Gauda, great-great-great-grandson of King Masinissa, Duumvir, Quinquenovalis, Patron; The Colonists'. He died at the age of seventy-seven after a reign of fifty years, and was obviously held in great esteem. His kingdom then passed to his only son Ptolemy who was a youth in his twenties, and about the same age as his father had been when he was given Mauretania by Augustus. Tacitus does not speak well of him and considered him 'Debauched and lazy'.

At a later date the young Ptolemy visited Rome, where Caligula took great exception to his flamboyance and became so jealous of his opulent display of wealth that he promptly had him murdered and annexed the

9 Obverse of a silver denarius with the portrait of the young king Juba II of Mauretania, 25 BC–AD 23.

Kingdom. This only instigated a further succession of riots on the part of the Moors and it was left to the Emperor Claudius to resolve the situation and to restore order under Seutonius Paulinus, who succeeded in chasing the dissidents into the desert. Paulinus found that his men could not stand the intense heat which, coupled with the meagre supplies of water and their heavy equipment, gave him no option but to withdraw. The tribes had, however, learnt their lesson.

10 *An elegantly shaped ornamental pool in a villa at Volubilis.*

Volubilis

Like most Roman towns the site of Volubilis was impeccable. It was built in the fertile plains at the foot of the Djerbel-Zerhoun hills and had a perpetual water supply from the local springs as well as from the Fertassa rivulet which still flows into the Khoumane Valley to the west. In common with some of the other North African towns it had to contend with the unwelcome attentions of the local tribes, which in this case were the troublesome Baquantes. They were often belligerent and whenever it pleased them they broke the many treaties that were made between them.

   The town was notable for the spacious and beautiful villas within its precincts which could rank amongst the most elegant in North Africa. Obviously a town of the well-to-do, the villas were built in the Pompeian style with rooms opening on to an atrium with an impluvium (*Ills. 10, 11*). Some villas even had their own oil presses at the rear. Many of the mosaic

floors are still *in situ* and some show the contemporary fauna, including the elephant. Others depict scenes from Greek mythology and one in particular shows a chariot race, the chariots being drawn by ducks.

The main industry must have been the production of olive oil, for here there are the substantial remains of the factory, the presses, the stripping mill for the olives and the settling vats. Oil was an essential commodity in the ancient world; amongst its many uses, it was the fuel used in the terracotta lamps which were to be found in all the cities and hamlets of the Empire from Asia Minor to Britain. Some moulds for these lamps with various designs, together with moulds for bowls, dishes and plates have been found near El Djem, Tunisia, where there must have been large pottery factories for their production.

The Triumphal Arch was built about AD 200 with an inscription dedicated to Caracalla (*Ill. 12*). But quite the most splendid finds are the bronzes from the villas (*Ill. 13*), which were cast by local artists and craftsmen, who were no doubt encouraged by the patronage of Juba. Undoubtedly it was a town where life was pleasant and relaxed, with its broad streets, its arcades of shops, and its Forum flanked by a handsome Capitol (Plate 1) with the law courts on the one side (Plate 2), and a central bakery on the other. There are, however, no signs of a theatre, amphitheatre or stadium and this seems to give the site the feeling that one has in a quiet and respectable old English country town. It is sad that by the end of the century the activities of the Baquantes had brought

11 *A rectangular pool in the court of a villa at Volubilis, showing the entrances to rooms beneath a colonnaded portico.*

about its evacuation and, although it was half-heartedly occupied by Jews and Christians at a later date, it never regained its former character.

Two particularly interesting inscriptions have come from Volubilis, the longer one reading, 'To Tiberius Claudius Caesar Augustus, son of a God, Pontifex Maximus, in his fourth year of tribunician power, imperator eight times: father of his country, the municipality of Volubilis having sought and gained Roman citizenship and connubium and remission of works, given by the decree of the decurions. Marcus Fadius Celer Flavianus Maximus, procurator of Augustus, pro-legate, made the dedication'. The other dedication was made in the time of Claudius, probably after he had taken over Mauretania, and it was to a 'Marcus Valerius Severus' of the tribe Galeria. Amongst his other titles he was a suffete or magistrate and the dedication was made by his wife, 'Fabia Bira, daughter of Izelta to her most indulgent husband. She put it up at her own expense to record the honour bestowed on him by the municipality of Volubilis for his services to the State'.

Two years before Augustus died in Rome in AD 14, the nomad tribes of the Musulamii raised a rebellion. They were led by Tacfarinas, an African who had joined the Third Augustan Legion as an auxiliary recruit and then deserted. Taking advantage of the training he had gained with the legion, he organised the haphazard activities of the Musulamii into disciplined units and persuaded the neighbouring tribes to join the uprising, thus posing a dangerous threat to the stability of Numidia.

12 *The single-span Triumphal Arch of Caracalla at Volubilis, built about AD 220. Compare with the far more grandiose example of the same emperor at Djemila, Plate 15.*

Having a detailed knowledge of the deserts and the surrounding country, they employed 'hit and run' tactics, vanishing as quickly as they appeared. Tacfarinas endeavoured to blackmail Tiberius in Rome to grant him land in exchange for the cessation of hostilities. The reaction of Tiberius, however, was to instruct the legion to change their tactics and become more mobile. This, however, did little to alter the situation, which remained in a state of flux up to the death of Juba.

The Moors of Mauretania had become very disenchanted with the rule of Juba II's son Ptolemy, and many joined Tacfarinas, influenced by his shrewd propaganda. Luckily for Mauretania, the proconsul for the year was Dollabella, who was very able and astute. He took the initiative, much against the will of the idle Ptolemy, and early one morning attacked the tribes where they had concentrated at Auzea, decimated them, and killed Tacfarinas. It was the end of seven years' upheaval and though there were a few periods of subsequent unrest, none were so damaging or lasting. An inscription at Oea dedicated to Augustus reads, 'To Augustus, Victory, Publius Cornelius Dollabella Consul, one of the seven feasts, Sodalis Titiensis, proconsul, Tacfarinas having been killed, set this up'. After years of guerrilla warfare, the Third Augustan Legion could now relax a little.

During the reign of Hadrian, and in the following years, the tribes of north Africa were becoming more integrated into Roman society; many of them, or the descendants of their intermarriage, were achieving distinction, especially in law. Their good education was possibly due in the first place to teachers at Carthage University, such as Sulpicius Apollonius, who had had the added distinction of tutoring the Emperor Pertinax when he was a boy. Pertinax too was of North African stock.

Hadrian was certainly one of the more itinerant of the Roman Emperors, and during his term of office had visited most areas of the Empire. After building his 'Wall' in Britain about AD 122 he left for Spain and then went on to Mauretania. It was a visit of short duration, but he could have at this time initiated the building of the stone boundary wall on the Numidian frontier. His other visit to Africa took place in AD 130–31 (*Ill. 14*). There had been in Africa over the previous five years a severe drought, which miraculously broke with torrential rains on his arrival. It was such a dramatic coincidence that he was at once accredited with having supernatural powers and was subsequently hailed by all as a god. During these visits he did much to improve the lot of the country as a whole, building roads and initiating other projects, as well as visiting the Third Augustan Legion to improve their morale and commend them on their past record.

Rome was fortunate in his two successors, the Emperors Antoninus Pius and Marcus Aurelius, the Antonines. It was Hadrian who appointed Marcus Cornelius Fronto, one of the most able lawyers in Rome, to be the tutor to the two adopted sons of Antoninus Pius, whom he had designated to be his heir. Fronto was born in North Africa at Cirta (Constantine), a popular city in the early years for Italian immigrants, and his origin could no doubt be traced to that period, although he did in fact

13 *A fine example of a bronze statue of an ephebe, young man, possibly an athlete, wearing a leafy diadem in his hair. Some remarkable bronzes have been recovered from the villas of Volubilis, evidence of the cultured taste of their owners. Rabat Museum.*

lay claim to a part Berber ancestry. He was a graduate of Carthage University who, as a young man in his early twenties, was called to the Bar in Rome where he became one of their leading advocates. However in spite of his great ability he was inclined to be very pedantic, and especially particular over the 'mot juste'.

14 *Silver denarius of Hadrian commemorating his visit to Africa in AD 130–131. On the reverse is a personification of Africa wearing an elephant skin head-dress and holding a cornucopiae and a scorpion.*

In AD 143 Fronto was appointed consul and throughout his life remained one of the greatest friends of Marcus Aurelius, a fact borne out by their correspondence, which still exists. Amongst the topics they discussed, the one which seems to have been given the most attention related to the state of their bowels! There is in Pompeii a small, attractive, and well preserved villa which has a painting on the garden wall of lions in a North African landscape. Though a little damaged it still has bright colour and is of particular interest because at the time of the eruption of Vesuvius in AD 79 it belonged to a Marcus Lucretius Fronto. The age of Lucretius Fronto at the time of the catastrophe is not known, but at least two generations must have elapsed between his generation and that of Cornelius Fronto. The similarity between the two names must indicate a family connection with North Africa, and Lucretius Fronto may well have had his origins in Cirta, hence the painting on the garden wall.

During the Antonine period there were few skirmishes in North Africa and the combined administrations were chiefly marked for tolerance and lack of excessive cruelty. Unfortunately for the Romans this was to change on the death of Marcus Aurelius and for the next two years the Empire was to plunge to the depths. He had decreed that his son Commodus should succeed him, which in due course he did at the age of eighteen. Marcus Aurelius thought very highly of his son, who showed him to his face a filial and dutiful demeanour. However, this was far from the truth; he was dissolute, debauched and cruel. It is related that when only twelve years old, because his bath water was not hot, he gave orders that the stoker of the furnace be cast into his own fires – to give the impression that this had been done, a sheep skin was thrown in by the attendants.

Six months after the death of his father, on 22 October AD 180, Commodus celebrated an imaginary victory over the German tribes. The Triumph which he held was, even for the Romans who were used to such spectacles, a unique event. According to Aelius Lampridius, who wrote his biography, he had with him in the chariot his favourite catamite, whom he fervently kissed throughout the occasion. Things went from bad to worse. In order to be free to indulge in his various unsavoury pursuits, he handed the government over to Perennius, who promptly lined his own pockets with the estates and fortunes of those he could conveniently do away with. Commodus too was not above this and was also responsible for the demise of a long list of ex-consuls, consuls and others of wealth and note.

In AD 190, due to widespread 'fiddling' on the part of those officials who were concerned with the grain supply to Rome, a famine broke out in the city. To prevent any further occurrences of this nature, or shortages due to crop failures in Egypt, Commodus organised a fleet of ships called the Commodiana Herculea to operate from Carthage with a reserve grain supply, and Carthage itself was renamed Alexandria Commodiana Togata. It was probably the only really constructive thing that he did whilst he was in power.

Amongst his many wantons, both male and female, Commodus had a favourite mistress, Marcia, whom he liked to dress as an Amazon. But by now he was becoming so eccentric that she and Quintus Aemilius Laetus, the Prefect of the Praetorian Guard, were becoming more and more apprehensive as to their own safety. The situation came to a head on New Year's Eve, AD 193. New Year's Day was a public holiday made significant by the traditional meeting of the Senate to appoint the new consuls for their yearly term of office. Commodus had decided to go to the function dressed as a gladiator, with a retinue of gladiators in attendance. It was a proposal that the Senate regarded with horror – he might just as well have considered going to a Royal Garden Party at Buckingham Palace in the same fancy dress. Marcia attempted to dissuade him, but he was adamant and after a heated argument he went to the baths. She then discovered that her name and that of Laetus were both included in the list of those to be executed the next day, so they hastily arranged for Commodus to be murdered when he returned for his evening meal. This she poisoned, but as he appeared to be recovering, she had him strangled by Narcissus, one of the palace staff. Laetus informed the Senate, who were thankful to be rid of him but, in view of the fact that he had been popular with the Guard, a notice was given out at the barracks that he had died from a stroke after his meal. The Senate then quickly elected Pertinax as Emperor in order to prevent any action on the part of the Guard.

Publius Helvius Pertinax was sixty, had been educated by Sulpicius Apollonius of Carthage, and had had a distinguished career. His mother was of North African stock, which meant that his background was not in reality aristocratic enough to fit him for the highest office, but in the circumstances the Senate had no option and could do little else. He had held commands in Britain, Syria and Dacia and had become very wealthy by the usual devious means. He had also held the post of Proconsul in Africa and in AD 192 Commodus had made him consul for the second time. To give him his due, he had twice endeavoured to decline the appointment of Emperor, but on New Year's Day, after he had been appointed by the Senate, he was presented to the Guard at the barracks. At the time the Guard were surly, for they had got on well with Commodus and consequently viewed the situation with suspicion. Pertinax's opening speech to them, which hinted at certain reforms, was therefore received with little enthusiasm.

After he had been elected, Pertinax found that, in order to pay for his extravagant lifestyle, Commodus had drained the Treasury. In order to pay the Guard their donatives, Pertinax had to sell off all the valuable private belongings that Commodus had accumulated. When this source was exhausted, he had no other recourse but to reduce their pay and this decision again caused a great deal of unrest in the barracks. The position had not been improved by several members of the Senate; Farco, for one, with the support of some of the other senators, violently opposed Pertinax on account of his plebian background and endeavoured to depose him. However the coup failed and those of the Guard who had supported the movement were executed. The remainder of the Guard at once revolted and marched on the palace and when Pertinax came out to meet them in the courtyard they murdered him and then returned to their barracks with his head on a spear. He had been Emperor for just eighty-seven days.

The authority now rested with the Praetorian Guard and the Senate could do little. The Guard's only concern was to elect an Emperor wealthy enough to ensure their support and pay their donatives, so they auctioned the Empire to the highest bidder. Flavius Sulpicianus and Didius Julianus were the two contestants. Didius had connections with Africa and his maternal grandfather had come from Cirta. He also had had a distinguished career and he too, by one way or another, had managed to amass great wealth. Like Pertinax, he had at one time been the Proconsul in Africa and had been Governor in Belgium and Dalmatia; he was duly elected by the Guard when he offered the highest bid.

At the time of Didius Julianus' accession there were three major armies stationed in the provinces. One was in Britain under Clodius Albinus, whose aristocratic family also came from Cirta in Africa; Septimius Severus, who was the commander of the troops in Upper Pannonia and a native of Leptis Magna in Libya, and Percennius Niger in Syria. None of these three commanders or their armies accepted Didius and regarded the action taken by the Praetorian Guard as unforgivable; each of the three armies wished to elect its own commander as Emperor. Severus was the nearest to Rome and set out at once for the capital, marching at the head of his men. Niger in Syria, however, was the favourite from the Senate's point of view for Syria was a wealthy colony, and the senators were considering the possible advantages it could have on their pockets should he become Emperor. Severus too was considered to be something of an upstart with a not very acceptable background. But Dio, the historian, did not support them because he thought Niger to be politically inept; an estimation borne out by the fact that Niger appeared to be in no hurry to leave the delights of Antioch, thinking he had only to appear in Rome to be elected.

Severus, in order to keep Albinus in Britain and to placate him, named him Emperor Designate and as he advanced on Rome, Didius lapsed into a state of panic. He had foolishly not paid the Guard the balance of the agreed price for the Empire and had thus lost their support. In an effort to regain their sympathy, he had their Prefect, Laetus, and Marcia executed for the murder of Commodus, but by now this had little impact. As a last resort, he offered to share the Empire with Severus, who refused. When he entered Rome, the Senate, in an endeavour to save face and to make the best of the situation, condemned Didius to death. He was executed in the Palace on 1 June AD 193, having been Emperor for two months and five days; Severus was elected in his place.

5

Septimius Severus and the Severan Dynasty

According to Dio, Septimius Severus was born in Leptis on 11 April AD 145. His father was of equestrian rank and the family were prosperous plebians who had the advantage of Roman citizenship long before Trajan had granted it to all the inhabitants when he raised the city to the state of Colonia. The family, however, was not regarded as having a sufficiently aristocratic background to warrant any members being elected to the Senate. Severus learnt Latin and Greek at school and spoke with a North African Punic accent, which he retained throughout his life. Dio says he was of small stature though powerfully built, but even when Emperor he dressed carelessly and was often untidy. He had a striking face with a mass of curly hair and the portrait head of him in the museum at Djemila is very possibly as true a likeness as any (Plate 13).

At eighteen Severus went to study in Rome. There he met two of his father's cousins, both having done well for themselves in the City, for this branch of the family had obtained influence and Senatorial rank. With their help and the goodwill of the Emperor, Marcus Aurelius, he also was granted the right to wear the purple toga. Life in Rome had not been all plain sailing for, like many others of the nobility, he had sown a few wild oats and was unfortunate enough to be charged at one time with adultery. He was, however, sufficiently confident at the hearing to conduct his own defence. This must have been convincing for he was lucky enough to be acquitted by Salvianus Julianus. Julianus was an eminent lawyer from Sousse and a contemporary of Cornelius Fronto, who at one time during his career was the director of one of the leading law schools in Rome. He was later on given the governorship of Germany, to be followed by that of Spain and, finally, in AD 168–169 he was appointed Proconsul in Africa, his homeland.

In AD 174 Severus was appointed Legate to the then Proconsul of North Africa and in his early years was very conscious of the dignity of the position which he held. On one official occasion when he was Legate and walking in a procession through Leptis, preceded by the lictors and fasces, he was hailed by an old acquaintance who rushed up to him and embraced him. Severus was not amused, for his dignity had been affronted and he had the man seized, led off and flogged. Later on an edict was published stating that: 'No plebian may embrace a Legate of the Roman people with impunity', and from that time on legates rode in a chariot to all official functions.

Before Marcus Aurelius died he made Severus a Tribune of the Plebs and it was then that he married Paccia Marciana, a girl from Leptis. Very little is known about her apart from the fact that she had two daughters. The date of her death is also uncertain, but it must have occurred before AD 185. On becoming Emperor, he built a memorial to her in Cirta and at the same time he set one up to his father who had left Leptis for Cirta some years previously and had died there.

Severus had commanded the legions in Syria during the governorship of Pertinax and it would seem that whilst on this tour of duty he became acquainted with the family of the young Julia Domna, who was subsequently to become his second wife. For some reason or other, after the death of Marcus Aurelius, Severus and Pertinax fell out of favour with Commodus. Severus therefore went to Athens, well out of the way, whilst Pertinax retired quietly to his estates south of Rome, where he remained until he was recalled by the Senate after the death of Commodus. Severus, however, was brought back from Athens by Commodus and made Legate of Lyon, but by now Marciana had died and Severus, remembering Julia Domna in Syria, decided to remarry. He had always been interested in horoscopes and when he studied Julia's he found it exceptional and favourable. But, possibly much more to the point, she was willing and the family was very wealthy.

Julia Domna was the daughter of Bassianus, the High Priest of the ancient town of Emesa, the present day Homs on the Orontes. Before Rome took Syria, Emesa was a city state, the High Priest being the hereditary ruler. However, during the second century AD under the Romans, the family retained only the priesthood and their inherited wealth. The religion centred around a large black stone, a meteorite that was sacred and kept in the temple. One of the old established religious rites, still practised in Julia's day, concerned the young girls of the city. On attaining puberty, they were required to kneel naked at the foot of the stone until they had been deflowered by any passer-by who happened to look in at the time; the theory being that those who were fortunate enough were acting by proxy for the god. The Syrian religions had numerous deities associated with stones, woods and water. It was from this source that the worship of the god Moloch with the accompanying rites of child sacrifice by fire passed to Carthage, rites which were by this stage forbidden by Rome.

Julia was sixteen when she married Severus in AD 187, and she gave birth to Caracalla the following year at Lyon. In spite of, or because of, her pagan upbringing she showed a remarkable religious tolerance, which was confirmed by Tertullian; she even employed a Christian girl as a nurse, one of the many Christians she subsequently employed in her households. She had a wider sensibility for the arts than Severus and filled her salon with the literary talent of the day. She admired Galen, who was now an old man and who had, after leaving the medical school at Pergamum, become the personal physican to Marcus Aurelius. He not only wrote treatises on medicine but also works on philosophy. Philostratus wrote for her *The Life of Apollonius* which was not completed until after her death, and the poets Oppian and Aelian were also contemporaries who figured in her circle.

In AD 189 Severus was appointed Governor of Sicily and it was here that Julia gave birth to Geta. The story is told that on the day he was born a hen from a local farm laid a purple egg, which was brought to her as an omen. When she gave it to Caracalla to look at, he promptly dropped and broke it, whereupon she accused him of fratricide, an omen which was obviously concocted and put about after the actual murder of Geta by his brother Caracalla. Severus did not stay long in Sicily. A fellow North African from Leptis, Aemelius Laetus, who was then Prefect of the Praetorian Guard, arranged in AD 191 for his transfer to the command of the legions in Upper Pannonia; this was the same Laetus executed by Didius for the murder of Commodus.

Severus' first act on becoming Emperor in AD 193 was to deify Pertinax, give him a state funeral and execute his murderers. He then fined heavily those senators who had supported Niger and summarily dealt with the Praetorian Guard. He ordered them to parade in front of their barracks without weapons, ostensibly to celebrate his appointment as Emperor, but when they were assembled, he denounced them for their treachery and banished them from Rome, his troops from Pannonia then moving in and preventing them from returning to the barracks to collect their belongings; they themselves then reformed the Guard.

In July of AD 193 Severus left for Syria and defeated Niger on the Plains of Issus near Antioch, heavily fining the cities of Nablus in Palestine and Antioch itself for giving Niger their support. He returned to Italy and on 17 February AD 197, defeated Albinus at Lyon. On hearing that Severus had declared his son Caracalla his successor with the title of Caesar, thus negating their original agreement, Albinus had come with his legions from Britain to depose him and, with the help of the Senate, be proclaimed Emperor. Instead he lost his life and Severus exhibited his head to the Senate in Rome. Amongst the effects of Albinus, Severus found numerous letters incriminating a number of the senators who had supported Albinus. On his return to Rome, to their consternation, he read back to the Senate one of their edicts which had, in fact, congratulated one of them, namely Clodius Celsinus from Sousse, for giving this support. Twenty-five senators lost their lives, as did the families of Albinus and Niger, and by these acts Severus established his sole authority over the Senate and the Empire.

It was probably about this time that Severus' sister and nephew arrived in Rome from Leptis, quite suddenly and without any previous warning of their intended visit. They proved to be a great embarrassment to the Imperial Household, for she could speak very little Latin, and that with an atrocious accent, had no social graces to speak of, and behaved like a peasant among the élite of Rome. The boy was little better and was at best awkward and uncouth. The two of them became such a laughing stock amongst the aristocracy that Severus was forced, as quickly as was decently possible, to pack them off back to Leptis. Apart from the fact that his nephew died soon after, nothing more was heard or has been recorded of them.

In the autumn of AD 197, the same year in which the abrasive Tertullian of the Christian Church in North Africa published his *Apologia* in Carthage, Severus returned to Syria with Julia, her sister Maesa, and the two boys, to continue his campaigns against the Parthians in the East. These were only partially successful, the highlight being the victory at Ctesiphon on 28 June AD 198. Caracalla by now was ten and Geta a little younger. To give the legions a rest from the rigours they had undergone, the family all returned to Antioch, where he distributed donatives to the men, before he, together with Julia, went on to Egypt. In Alexandria he cemented cordial relations with the Egyptians by instituting a number of reforms which were long overdue and welcomed by them, but his real intent was to secure the grain supply to Rome. From there, in AD 199, they toured the antiquities of Upper Egypt, sailing down the Nile to Thebes, where he had repairs carried out on the great statues of Amenophis III, the Colossi of Memnon (who were never heard to make their famous 'moaning' noise again).

On New Year's Day, AD 202, the Imperial family were back in Antioch where Caracalla assumed the Toga of Manhood and was appointed consul for the year, an appointment which he held jointly with Severus. On their return to Rome, they celebrated the victory at Ctesiphon with a Triumph and the building of the Arch of Severus, which still stands near the Senate House in the Roman Forum. Whilst he had been in Upper Egypt, Severus had had the misfortune to contract diphtheria which, after his recovery, left him with a painful arthritis. Caracalla therefore had to deputise for him in any lengthy processions. It was a disability that was to remain with him for the rest of his life but, disregarding it, he later, in the year AD 202, left Rome again with Julia for North Africa and his home town of Leptis Magna, where he began a programme of improvements which embellished the city with some of the most outstanding buildings and architecture to be found in North Africa and the Empire.

Many North Africans rose to prominent positions of authority under Severus, but none was more notorious than Fulvius Plautianus who had been a boyhood companion of the Emperor's during his youth in Leptis. Severus appointed him to the office of Praetorian Prefect and his first task was to apprehend the wife and daughter of Niger and hand them over into the custody of Julia, to look after as hostages whilst he was away in Syria.

Plautianus rapidly became the most disliked and influential character in Rome, for in the eyes of Severus he could do no wrong. It seemed that Severus felt an almost unnatural attachment for him and there is no doubt that Plautianus exploited it to the utmost. In common with many confidants of the various other emperors he amassed incalculable wealth, even during the first year of office, and his lifestyle far outshone that of Severus himself. One of his foibles was to keep a herd of zebras that he had arranged to be shipped specially from North Africa just to inflate his ego. Dio records that on official journeys he occupied the best accommodation available and ordered the finest food, to the extent that once when Severus fancied some mullet for his supper, one of his favourite dishes, he found that Plautianus had stripped the market and he had to beg a few as a favour.

Severus was not ostentatious and his daily routine was almost Spartan. He arose at dawn and after a walk heard cases in court until midday. He then had a light snack which was followed by more work and after this he had a bath which was followed by the evening meal; he disliked banquets and would try to avoid them at all costs. The excesses of Plautianus went from strength to strength. Those walking on the streets of Rome were expected to step aside as he passed; he even insisted that all the males on his household staff had to be castrated, whatever their age. It is a wonder he was able to employ anybody. His final accolade was to persuade Severus to arrange a marriage between his daughter Plautilla and Caracalla. The wedding was so splendid that it bordered on a Triumph, but he had not reckoned with Caracalla, who had been very difficult of late and who after the ceremony refused to have anything to do with his bride. Both he and Julia heartily disliked Plautianus for the influence he wielded. The feeling was mutual, for Plautianus did his utmost, whenever he had the opportunity, to discredit Julia with accusations of adultery. He even went to the extent of torturing her attendants in an effort to obtain evidence, for Julia unfortunately had a reputation for being promiscuous. However it would appear that, in spite of his efforts, no case could be proven against her.

Whilst they were in North Africa, Julia Domna lost no time in getting her own back, for she noticed and pointed out to Severus that the statues in Leptis that had been raised to Plautianus were more resplendent and far outnumbered those that were dedicated to Severus himself. More-over, Plautianus had included himself in groups which should have been devoted entirely to Severus and his family. This was too much even for Severus and the bronzes were removed and melted down forthwith. Plautianus himself became increasingly aware of the coolness and displeasure which Severus now showed in his dealings with him; for Plautianus this was a very unusual experience.

It was not long after the return to Italy that Severus' brother, Septimius Geta, died in Rome. He had always remained quietly in the background and though he had held several distinguished appointments, he had kept his opinions to himself and not intruded into State affairs. However, when he was dying, he warned Severus against Plautianus whom he thought, from rumours that he had heard, was preparing a coup d'état. Plautianus had in fact realised that Severus, now past sixty, was not in good health and that Caracalla, when he became Emperor, would exact revenge for his unwanted marriage. To forestall such an event Plautianus arranged with Saturnius, who was a Syrian and an officer commanding the palace guard, to murder Severus in his room when he was next on duty, then Caracalla, and after this had been done, to send for him so that he could be proclaimed Emperor in the palace.

Saturnius at once reported the whole plan to Severus and Caracalla and they set a trap by sending word at the right moment to Plautianus that the murders had taken place. He hurried to the palace and, to his shock and confusion, found them both still alive. During the ensuing argument, Caracalla stabbed him and had his body thrown into the street. Plautilla was with Julia when this occurred and Caracalla lost no time in telling her with great pleasure of her father's death. Within a very short space of time, he had divorced her and banished her to the Lipari Islands with her brother.

The historian Dio Cassius was a member of the Senate during the reign of Severus and was present on the following day when Severus gave an account of the murder. He first began by blaming himself for having allowed Plautianus too much power, but he then made it quite clear that as far as he was concerned, other members of the Senate had been implicated in the plot. The atmosphere in the Senate at this point must have become quite electric; many of those present shifted uneasily in their seats and one or two tried to slide out quietly. Dio gives an account of the purge that followed. Apparently an informer had given evidence that he had seen a bald senator attending some clandestine meetings and Dio relates how during the Emperor's harangue they all eyed each other to assess the degree of baldness of those present. He himself, he states, involuntarily put his hand to his head to reassure himself that no hair had gone missing and that he still had his full quota. The indictment, however, went on to say that the individual concerned wore the striped toga of a magistrate, which immediately narrowed the field. Unfortunately for him, there was sitting in the Senate a magistrate called Baebus Marcellinus, whose bald pate shone out like a beacon amongst the heads of his contemporaries, and all eyes turned to him. He, to escape censure and hoping for the best, demanded the equivalent of an identity parade. The informer was brought in and, according to Dio, he looked hesitantly around, not being able to pick anyone out until an enemy of Marcellinus indicated to him where he was sitting. He was then hauled from the Senate and just had time to say goodbye to his wife and children who were waiting in the crowds outside, before he was led away and summarily decapitated. After the furore had died down, Severus calmed the situation by appointing Papinian, Rome's most prominent jurist, to the office of Praetorian Prefect. This divorced the post from its previous military connotations and brought it more into line with the civil administration. It also reduced the ever present threat of rebellion on the part of the Praetorian Guard itself.

Severus died in York on 4 February AD 211, in the palace that he had had built in the legion's headquarters there, the foundations of which lie beneath the present Minster. He had gone to Britain in AD 208 with Julia, Caracalla, Geta and Papinian, in an effort to settle the long-standing unrest that still existed with the Caledonians beyond Hadrian's Wall. He had given Geta the title of Augustus, which made him equal in rank with Caracalla, an act which did nothing to improve the bitter quarrelling and the hostility that existed between the brothers. On his deathbed he left the Empire between them as joint Emperors, with the words: 'Keep the peace between you, look after the army and disregard all else'. He also left Rome, the Treasury and the Empire, especially North Africa, considerably better off than when he took office, in spite of having debased the currency.

Back in Rome, Caracalla and Geta divided the palace between them and lived separately, but all efforts at bringing about a reconciliation between them failed. In the end Caracalla let it be known to his mother that he would like to meet her, together with his brother, in her apartments to effect an improvement in their relations. This turned out to be nothing but a ruse on the part of Caracalla for shortly after his arrival he murdered Geta in Julia's arms. His hatred for his brother was completely pathological. He informed the Senate that he had acted in self-defence and he then proceeded to do away with all Geta's friends and acquaintances, both male and female, including those friends of Julia's who openly mourned him. Amongst them was Cornuficia, the only surviving daughter of Marcus Aurelius, Julia's closest friend who, though she was elderly, was compelled to commit suicide. His vengeance was such that it even extended to Sammonicus Serenus, whom he did not know personally, but who had written a book, the *Rerum Reconditarum Serenus Libri*, a copy of which Caracalla found in Geta's rooms, so he too was done away with.

Plautilla and her brother who were living quietly on the Lipari Islands were also murdered. Dio further records that the holocaust was not confined to Italy but extended to the colonies, where thousands, many of them of exalted rank, lost their lives. It was Papinian, though, who was the greatest loss to Rome. When asked by Caracalla to attest to the legality of his accession, he replied that 'fratricide was easier to commit than to defend', an answer which cost him his life.

Caracalla did little for Africa in a direct way and was detested by the Senate and the citizens of Rome, but the country did benefit from his edict of AD 212, which conferred Roman citizenship upon all subjects of the Empire. This act of legislation passed in AD 212–13 was called the 'Constitutio Antoniniana' and was one of the most significant to be passed in Roman history. The decree gave all the provincial governors criminal jurisdiction over their citizens, but the taxes to which they were all liable were raised from five to ten per cent.

Most of Caracalla's time as Emperor was spent with the legions with whom he was popular, and when they were away on campaigns, Julia acted as Regent. On his last journey to Edessa, he crossed the bridge that his father had built over the Cendere river in Commagene when he went on his first journey to the East, just after he had been made Emperor. At each corner of the bridge Severus had set up a column and had dedicated all four of them, one to Julia, one to Caracalla, one to Geta, and the last, which carried his inscription, to himself. On his way east, Caracalla knocked down the column dedicated to Geta and the pieces are still there. He made Edessa his headquarters, as his father had done, and then one day decided to visit Carrhae with a small party to attend the sacrifices to the Moon Goddess which took place on the seventh of the month. On his way there he was murdered by Martialus on the orders of Macrinus, a Moor from Mauretania, who was then the Prefect of the Guard. Macrinus had not got on well with Caracalla who considered him to be effeminate and was not slow in taunting him maliciously about it. Macrinus enlisted the support of the Senate for his plans to remove Caracalla, for they had no love for him either. The opportunity occurred on this journey – Caracalla had not been well and when he went apart from the rest to relieve himself he was stabbed by Martialus, one of the legionaries, who had followed him on some pretext. He too was immediately killed by those of the bodyguard who were loyal to Caracalla. After his death, Macrinus became the first and only Moor to be elected Emperor by the Senate, even though he had never himself attained Senatorial rank. He also lost his life not long after, in AD 218, near Antioch.

Julia had gone from Rome to Antioch a sick woman; it is thought that she had developed cancer of the breast and could no longer contend with the swiftly changing politics of the Empire. To avoid any confrontation with Macrinus, and having lost her husband and sons, she commited suicide by starving herself to death.

Two further members of the family were to become emperors before the end of the Dynasty, but neither of them did anything very constructive for Africa. Julia Soaemias, the daughter of Julia Maesa and the niece of Julia Domna, had a son, Elagabalus, who had succeeded to the office of High Priest at the Temple in Emesa, the position once held by Julia's father Bassianus. The legions in Syria, on the death of Macrinus, elected him Emperor, for they considered him to be the undoubted, albeit illegitimate, son of Caracalla, whose memory they still respected. Some years previously in Rome there had been a great scandal regarding an affair that Caracalla had had with his cousin, an affair that had culminated in the birth of a boy.

It proved to be another disaster for Rome and the Empire. Elagabalus was fond of outlandish dress and refused to wear the toga at important functions preferring to appear wearing a collection of necklaces and bracelets. He had arrived in Rome with the sacred black stone from the Temple at Emessa, which was possibly a meteorite and conical in shape, and had it installed in a temple built especially for it in the Capitol. He then decided that as it was the god of Emessa it should be wedded to the goddess Astarte of Carthage, and arrangements were made for her ancient image to be brought from Africa for the ceremony; a course of events which was heartily opposed by the Carthaginians. His idiosyncracies did not stop there. One of his favourite antics was to drive a chariot drawn by four naked girls about the public gardens and the palace grounds; to stimulate their performance he would flick their bare bottoms with a whip. At dinner parties in the palace he is said once to have seated his guests on air cushions concealed under the sumptious materials that covered the couches, and to have them punctured at the height of the meal to cause embarrassment to all concerned.

To begin with, some in Rome had found his antics amusing, but Dio and the Senate viewed them with distaste and they became even more bizarre. He scoured the colonies, chiefly Africa, for those virile enough to satisfy his sexual proclivities and went so far as to marry one, Zoticus, the son of a baker. The situation was serious due to the fact that these favourites were given important positions in the State and Zoticus, like Plautianus in the time of Severus, became very rich and powerful. He sold what the Romans referred to as 'smoke'. Those who desired Elagabulus to grant them a favour would approach Zoticus and pay him to bring their request to his notice. But of course nothing was done, their requests vanished into thin air and Zoticus pocketed the money.

By 13 March AD 222 the Guard had had enough. Although they were broad-minded, they did expect a certain degree of decorum from the Emperor. They descended on the palace, sought him out with his court and Zoticus, and killed them, dragging the Emperor's body through Rome before flinging it into the Tiber. He was just seventeen years old. His portraits on the coinage are flattering when compared with his marble portrait bust in the Capitoline Museum in Rome, a youth with a weak rounded face showing little resemblance to Caracalla, but he could have taken after his mother Soaemias.

Elagabalus was succeeded by his cousin Alexander Severus, son of Julia Mamaea, the sister of Julia Soaemias, and it was she who virtually ran the Empire with the help of the lawyer Ulpian. The character of Alexander was quite the opposite to that of Elagabalus. Apt to be cautious, Alexander did not like wasting money, a habit he may have acquired from his mother, for she kept a tight hold on to the privy purse in case the Praetorian Guard became restless and had to be appeased with a donative. He was inclined to be religious and his first priority was to return the stone to the Temple at Emesa and the statue of Astarte to Carthage. He is said to have kept shrines in the palace to all the cults in Rome, including that of Christianity. In this respect, he mentally wore a belt as well as braces and believed in keeping his options open.

Alexander's mother chose Barbia Orbiana, a girl from a very noble family, to be his wife but, later on, when the Senate awarded her the title of Augusta, which made her equal in rank with her mother-in-law, Mamaea became insanely jealous. In spite of his protests, for he was very fond of his wife, Mamaea made Alexander divorce her and Orbiana was forthwith banished to Africa. When her father also registered his protests Mamaea had him executed. There is a story that on one occasion visiting diplomats presented Orbiana with a magnificent set of pearl drop earrings, which Alexander considered too opulent for her to wear. He insisted on putting them up for auction in Rome and was puzzled because there were no bids, not having the wit to realise that no Roman matron would dare to wear jewellery forbidden to the Empress.

It was unfortunate that Severus Alexander was tied to his mother's apron strings but, even so, this did not deter him from going with the legions on a campaign to the east. This unfortunately did not achieve very much, but he was elected with Dio to be the joint consul in Rome for the years AD 229 and 234. His last campaign was with the legions on the Rhine. Here he made the mistake of endeavouring to bribe the tribes into a peaceful settlement, a course of action which created a great amount of dissent amongst the army staff. This fermented and was brought to a head by the Thracian, Maximinus, and eventually led to his murder, together with that of his mother, on 10 March AD 235. Their deaths marked the end of the Severan Dynasty and there is little to commemorate Alexander in Africa, apart from the Arch which was dedicated to him at Dougga and the fact that he promoted the city of Althinburos near Tebessa, which Hadrian had previously made a Municipium in AD 128, to the status of Colonia. The remains of this once large city have been described as a monumental mess – the only structure left standing being, once again, the Triumphal Arch. It was the end of the golden age in Africa, a period of relative peace and prosperity that had lasted for almost fifty years and was largely due to the influence of the Syrian princesses.

Maximinus was in power for three years before he died, but when he was alive he had to raise the money to increase the emoluments to the legions by way of severely increasing the taxes. These, as it happened, were levied very assiduously in North Africa, especially in the region of Thysdrus (El Djem). The local procurator had endeavoured to lay hands on the estates of the wealthy there, but the young heirs to these fortunes revolted and murdered the procurator.

The Proconsul at the time was Gordian, who was eighty years of age. On the death of Maximinus, who had also been murdered, he was elected together with his son to be the joint Emperor. Their term of office was to last only two months before the son was killed in a battle, followed by the suicide of Gordian, his father. It was Capellianus, the Governor of Numidia and Legate of the Third Augustan Legion, who had defeated the younger Gordian in battle. His victory resulted in many of the nobles in Carthage losing their lives, together with many of those others who had supported the Gordian family. It was the beginning of a period of anarchy and unrest in Africa up to the time of Diocletian, notable for a succession of short-lived Emperors and a period which was not helped by Gordian III, who disbanded the Third Augustan Legion for the part they had played in the deaths of his family. It was the beginning of the decline in the fortunes of North Africa.

6

Leptis Magna and Sabratha

Leptis Magna, Sabratha and Oea, the Tripoli of today, were the most important cities in Tripolitania during the Roman period. All three were of Punic origin and formed the Cities of the Tripolis, but were known as the Emporia. Leptis came under the jurisdiction of Carthage and had to pay a tax to that city, but Oea and Sabratha were administered locally by Leptis itself. However, after the fall of Carthage the cities came under the control of Numidia and were later, in 46 BC, incorporated into the Province of Africa Nova by Julius Caesar. By AD 106 they were being protected by a Roman garrison. During the Civil Wars Leptis had the misfortune to back the losing side and, in consequence, was reduced to stipendary status, as well as being compelled to send a heavy annual duty in olive oil to Rome, a vast amount that totalled three million pounds.

In 23 BC under Augustus, Leptis became part of the greater Province of Africa though it still retained its Punic constitution as far as the municipal administration was concerned. From this time on the city began to expand and develop, at first under the influence of Calpurnius Piso, a member of one of the most distinguished families in Rome which originally came into prominence after the battle of Carrae in 216 BC. An earlier member of the family was consul in 146 BC and took part in the Carthaginian wars.

Part of the economy was dependent on the olive groves which were established in the hinterland, and these were worked almost entirely with slave labour. Its other source of wealth was derived from the caravans of the Garamantes who brought to the coast from the interior gold, carbuncle stones, ivory, slaves and the many wild animals, including the ostrich, that one sees pictured in many of the wall paintings and mosaics. Leptis also exported the garum sauce made from the entrails of salted fish which the Romans considered to be a great delicacy.

The two ports were at Leptis and Oea. Although Sabratha was built right on the cost with views over the sea it had only been what amounted to a roadstead. The cities were protected from the desert by high jebels, beyond which lay the Oasis of Ghadames, the Cydame of the Romans.

This was at the junction of the Saharan trade routes and in its time a flourishing slave market – even today one can still see the rings to which they were tethered. During the Roman period it had an important fortified garrison which protected the coastal towns and the *limes*, a series of ditches covering a great expanse and stretching for miles to guard the boundaries against the desert tribes. As in Numidia, many of the farms were in the hills, some fortified, but all were protected by a string of lookout posts supported by two larger forts situated at El Garbia and Germa. These fortifications stretched to the west to the Chott Djerhid in Tunisia and further on into Numidia, covering some 1200 miles.

The first forty-four miles of road away from the coast were laid down by Auleus Lamia when Tiberius was Emperor and became known as the Via Lamia, the milestones being erected when Caracalla came to power. One of these stones still stands near the Severan Arch and records the distance in Roman miles. The new roads opened up the interior to the farmers and more extensive olive groves were planted, but these developments stirred up the Garamantes to increased agressive activity. This had to be dealt with by the Third Augustan Legion under Cornelius Balbus, who chased them into the desert well beyond Ghadames. In AD 69 the Garamantes again raided the outlying farms to the point of threatening Leptis itself and, once again, the Third Augustan Legion, now commanded by Valerius Festus, had to come to the rescue. Their energetic action forced the Garamantes to retire towards Ghadames with their booty, but Festus with detachments of the legion, using a route known to them as the Praetor Caput Saxi, cut them off, annihilated them and returned to Leptis having recovered the loot. One last incursion made by the Romans into the desert took place in AD 100 under Septimius Flaccus and Julius Maternus, this time with the co-operation of the Garamantes who knew the terrain. A truce must have taken place between them on this occasion, for the expedition penetrated right through the Sudan into Ethiopia, a very great distance across the deserts and no mean feat by any standards.

The buildings in Leptis fall into two periods, that of Augustus and that of Severus. The old Forum was the original centre of the town and was paved in 5 BC. Not long after AD 18 all the streets of the city were paved and the original dedication recording the work has been preserved, but it is rather verbose; it reads, 'To Tiberius Caesar Augustus, son of Augustus, grandson of divine Julius, pontifex maximus, consul 5 times, imperator 8 times, in his 37th year of tribunician power, Gaius Rubellius Blandus, Quaestor of divine Augustus, tribune of the plebs, praetor, consul, proconsul, priest, patron, from the revenues of the lands which he restored to the Lepticani had all the main roads of the state of Leptis paved with stone, Marcus Etrilius Lupercus, proconsul, praetorian legate, patron, auctioned the contracts for the work AD 18'.

The Cardo Maximus passed through the city from the Forum to the city gate, with side streets leading off from either side (*Ill. 15*). The two temples in the Forum were dedicated to Liber Pater and to Rome and Augustus, the latter being built in the reign of Tiberius. On the eastern

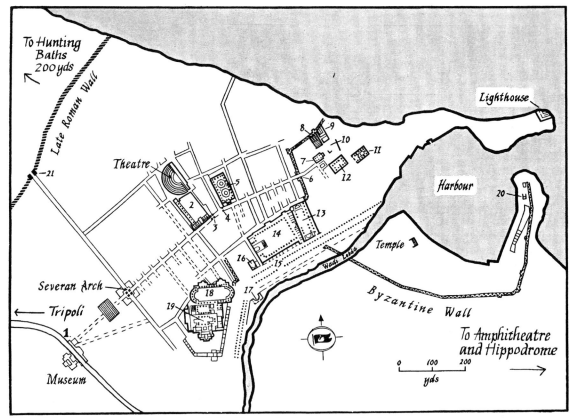

15 *Plan of Leptis Magna.* 1 *Entrance to excavations; 2 Chalcidicum; 3 Arch of Trajan; 4 Arch of Tiberius; 5 Market; 6 Byzantine Gate; 7 Old Forum Church; 8 Temple of Liber Pater; 9 Temple of Rome and Augustus; 10 Old Forum; 11 Curia, 12 Old Basilica; 13 Severan Basilica; 14 Severan Forum; 15 Colonnaded Street; 16 Christian Church; 17 Nymphaeum; 18 Palaestra; 19 Hadrianic Baths; 20 Doric Temple; 21 West Gate.*

side of the Forum one can see the old Basilica and adjacent to it the Curia, or Senate House. The outstanding features of the temples are the beautiful and well proportioned columns, especially in one small temple by the sea, where they are fashioned out of variegated marbles, each a different colour and turned in one piece, not set up in drum sections one on top of the other. The capitals and bases are worked in bright white marble which accentuates the colour of the columns, a feature very noticeable in the architecture of the North African cities. In AD 109 the Arch of Trajan was built of limestone to span the Cardo near the Chalcidicum to celebrate the raising of the city to the status of Colonia; at a later date a large amphitheatre was added away to the east of the town.

The superb baths were built in AD 126–27 by Hadrian and were almost as large as some of those in Rome, but they were more intimate and had a great deal of architectural detail (*Ill. 16*). At the entrance to the baths which leads into the complex is the seated figure of Mars (Plate 5). Here there are not only the usual changing rooms, palaestra, lavatories, hot and warm rooms, but also a large open-air and very elegant swimming pool. It is, however, the cold plunge that is the architectural gem; a large rectangular marble bath surrounded with graceful arches, and presiding over the pool the life-size statue of Antinous (Hadrian's favourite) as Apollo in unblemished white marble (Plate 7). It is not unlikely that the white marble statues of Apollo in the theatre date from this period.

Commodus was responsible for the final touches. He used a grey veined marble to face the walls, most of which has now been stripped away, no doubt for other building projects, but it has revealed the wonderful golden colour of the stone. An arch to commemorate Hadrian was put up across the Cardo not far from the one that had been erected to Trajan at an earlier date (*Ill. 17*).

Across the sand dunes a little way out of the city there is another small bath complex, with low domed roofs and built most probably for private use. Due to being completely covered by the sand dunes over the centuries it is very well preserved and the hypocaust system of the hot and warm rooms is practically intact. The walls of the frigidarium are covered with wall paintings of hunting scenes, one in particular showing a leopard hunt; for this reason they are known as the 'Hunting Baths'. Sir Mortimer Wheeler does not consider these baths to have been a public institution, but rather to have belonged to a guild of hunters who supplied the animals to the local amphitheatres. They could even have supplied the lions for Caesar's Triumph or, on the other hand, the baths could have been the prerogative of some other concern. From a house

16 *Swimming bath in the Hadrianic Baths at Leptis Magna, built in* AD *126–127. They are amongst the largest in the Roman world and noted for their architectural detail (see also Plates 5 and 7).*

not far away came the splendid fishing mosaic now in the Tripoli Museum (*Ill. 18*).

The two other outstanding features of the old town were the large Eastern Market and the theatre with its extensive views across the sea. A wealthy citizen of Leptis, Annobal Tapapius Rufus, built the market in 8 BC and donated it to his fellow citizens. It is very spacious and possibly the most impressive in North Africa today. In the centre are two splendid pavilions raised on a low platform and reached by a shallow wide flight of

18 *The mosaics from Roman North Africa are amongst the best preserved and most interesting from the empire. They are full of mythological subjects or daily life scenes depicted in great detail as here, two men fishing. The older man sits on a rock with his rod and line, baiting his hook, the younger has just caught a fish and is about to retrieve it in his scoop net. The mosaic was found in the 'Villa of the Nile', which was on the edge of the city near the harbour. Tripoli Museum.*

steps (*Ill. 19*). Between the columns of the pavilion there is still an intact stone counter, the butcher's slab with deep cut grooves, the result of sharpening knives over the years (*Ill. 20*). It is small detail which immediately brings the ruins to life and conjures up the shadows of those who thronged the market centuries ago. The whole area was once enclosed by a columned portico with shops, but here again there is another unusual feature; a bas relief of two ships carved on a plinth (*Ill. 21*), illustrative of those that crowded the quays and harbour in those days. One can still see engraved into a paving stone a small circular chequer board where games were played with dice or stones by the children, or possibly also by the adults. Similar games are found throughout the cities of the Empire and one can be seen in the courtyard of the synagogue at Capernaum.

When it was completed Rufus dedicated the market to Caesar Augustus. A Marcus Licinius Frugi was consul at the time and the dedication reads, after a preamble: 'Annobal Tapapius Rufus, son of Himilcho, suffeti, flamen, prefect of the sacred rites had this made at his own expense and also dedicated it'. Another smaller market was built and donated to the City by a private citizen in AD 11–12 and known as the 'Chalcidicum'. It was dedicated 'To the divinity of Imperator Caesar Augustus, son of a God, pontifex maximus, imperator 20 times, consul 13 times, in his 34th year of tribunician power, are dedicated the Chalcidicum and portico and the gate and the road'.

The theatre was also built by Tapapius Rufus, whose name suggests a Punic origin, and completed in AD 1. Though probably not so impressive or sophisticated as the one at Sabratha, it was more elegant. The graceful sweep of the auditorium looks onto the *scaena frons* backed by a broad colonnade, which served as a cool and airy ambulatory. Behind this colonnade was the temple dedicated to the Di Augusti. A seated figure of Niobe, carved in white marble, sits brooding over the theatre from the

19 *The market at Leptis Magna was built in 8 BC and given to the city by a wealthy citizen, Annobal Tapapius Rufus. There were two circular pavilions or kiosks in the centre, surrounded by an Ionic colonnade. The goods for sale were displayed on the broad-topped stone counters.*

20 *One of the stone counter tops in the market at Leptis Magna is deeply scored from knives being sharpened on it over countless years. It probably served as a butcher's slab.*

topmost tier of seats and looks across to the columns of the ambulatory with the deep blue sea beyond (Plate 4). Guarding either side of the stage are life-size statues of Apollo in white marble and nearby are the heads of the sacred Hermes on their pillars. The honey-coloured stone glows magically against the shadows cast by the evening light, so that one can hardly imagine a bawdy play, beloved by the Romans and vividly described by Apulieus in *The Golden Ass*, being played here, though it is recorded that on one occasion, Caracalla did permit his favourite actor to come to Leptis for a season.

The auditorium at Leptis is separated from the stage by a barrier of thin wide slabs of stone set up on end. On one of these slabs some wag of centuries ago, no doubt in a fit of boredom, has incised the lively graffito of a large head of a centurion (*Ill. 22*). Graffiti of antiquity are the one medium whereby the peoples of the past come closer to us. They span and shrink the years making one acutely aware of the fact that human nature has changed little. Pompeii and Herculaneum are rich in various graffiti which give a vivid insight into everyday life in the Roman cities of the first century AD, an existence halted in the space of a few hours by the eruption of Vesuvius. Who can resist the pictures brought to mind by that scribble on a street wall which says: 'Livia to Alexander, what do I care if your health is good, you can drop dead tomorrow as far as I'm concerned'; or the terse: 'Serena has had enough of Isidore'. The tavern landlords did not escape criticism either. One toper in disgust exclaims: 'May you landlord of the devil drown in your own piss wine – you keep the best bottles for yourself you swine'. Besides these, there were the jottings of the actors who stayed in the local pensions, usually above a wine shop. In one case the company of the pop star of the day, Actius

21 *In the market place at Leptis Magna is a four-arched base for a statue which, the fourth-century AD inscription records, was erected to one Porfyrius who had presented four elephants to the city. On two of the pillars are a pair of merchant ships finely carved in relief, no doubt an accurate representation of those that would have been a common sight in the nearby harbour.*

22 *An interesting graffito of a centurion has been scratched on one of the upright stone slabs that separated the stage and the auditorium in the theatre at Leptis Magna.*

Anicetus, records its stay. Did they, one wonders, tour the theatres of Africa? But there is one graffito that immortalises the stay of a famous doctor with a wealthy family in Herculaneum. Someone, possibly one of the servants, has written on the lavatory wall next to the kitchen: 'Apollinaris, physician to Titus, relieved himself here satisfactorily'.

Few graffiti of this calibre have survived in the cities of Africa. Time and weather have possibly obliterated them, but someone full of the joy of life has written on a step near the Forum in Timgad: 'To hunt, to bathe, to play, to laugh, that is the way to live'. It is noticeable that work is not mentioned. Others are to be seen on the columns of the library courtyard, but these in no way fall into the realm of classic literature. One final example must be mentioned, which also has its counterpart in Italy and is to be found on the arch in the middle of the ruins of Hammam Zouarka. It warns 'those who urinate here will incur the wrath of Mars'. This then was the city where Severus was born and brought up before he went to Rome. He returned for a lengthy visit with Julia Domna, Caracalla, and Geta in AD 202, providing the money for the many improvements he instituted and for the beautiful buildings that made the city one of the finest in North Africa.

Severus' first act on arrival was to exempt Leptis Magna from the land tax, but the taxes on the merchandise coming in by sea, and on the sale of slaves, were still collected. His second project was to improve the water supply. In all the North African cities a great quantity of water was required for the nymphaeums and the municipal baths. To increase the supply, he cut off the Cinyps river with a barrage (dam) to form a lake some twenty kilometres away from the city and the water was taken to Leptis through underground conduits which were controlled by sluices.

The course of the Wadi Lebda that flowed through the city was dredged out, and the harbour itself enlarged to a width of forty metres; the basin being protected from the sea by substantial ashlar blocks weighing a ton each. Large warehouses were erected on the wharves and the mole extended further out to protect the entrance which had a lighthouse on the extremity. Steps led down from the quays to the ships which were tied up to the harbour walls. In concept it was very modern, but the main difficulty was to keep the basin clear of the silt brought down by the river which in the years to come finally choked the harbour. In the early centuries it was a scene of great activity. All the luxuries brought in by the caravans, the gold, the gems and the ivory, were shipped to Rome. In the port of Ostia are the remains of an office in the Square of Corporations with a mosaic floor denoting that it was particularly concerned with the shipments from Leptis and the other North African ports.

This new harbour (*Ill. 23*) was considered by Sir Mortimer Wheeler not to have had a great deal of use, due to the fact that the berths used for tying up the shipping showed little sign of wear. Though this was probably the case there must have been a great amount of traffic to sustain the city's wealth and to export to Rome the vast amount of oil that Leptis had been fined at the end of the Civil Wars. The marble used by Commodus to clad the walls of Hadrian's baths must have come through the port, and it is not beyond the bounds of possibility that Sallust shipped the lions for Caesar's Triumph from here, also quite possibly some of the other exotic species brought in by the Garamantes for the amphitheatres. Even after the rebuilding there must have been an appreciable amount of trade throughout the Severan period.

The tremendous achievements, however, were the Severan Forum and the splendid Basilica housing the Law Courts and the city administration. Later on under the Byzantines, and with little alteration,

this became a Christian basilica and the pulpit that was set up at that time is still there in remarkably good condition. The Severan Forum was extensive, roughly rectangular in shape and approximately 100 by 60 metres. It was dominated at the south end by a majestic temple which, it is thought, must have been dedicated to the Severan family; the bases of the columns are unusual for, instead of being plain, they are decorated with carvings of mythological reliefs.

Around the Forum are the remains of arcades built with the same honey-coloured stone. The intersections of the arches were embellished with medallions, each carved with the head of Medusa (Plate 3), and these can rank as some of the finest examples of this motif. It was a popular decoration much used in the cities of Asia Minor such as Perge and Didyma near Ephesus, where a very large head has fallen from the temple of Apollo. At the end of the Forum and facing the temple are some of the shop fronts (Plate 6), and the entrance to the spacious vestibule leading to the Basilica. The door frames are in stone carved with an egg-and-cup design which can also be seen in the theatre at Perge. They are in perfect proportion and give a feeling of grandeur; and they are very reminiscent

23 *Leptis Magna's harbour covered 24 acres and was cut out of the end of the Wadi Lebda as it entered the sea. Unfortunately, for all its magnificence, its quays, warehouses, temple and lighthouse, it seems to have silted up fairly soon after completion since there are few signs of tell-tale rope wear on the stone mooring blocks.*

1 *Juba II's city at Volubilis, which he probably used as his western capital, was essentially a Hellenistic city that overlay the earlier Libyo-Punic settlement. The* *Capitol is typical of many erected throughout Roman North Africa, with elegant columns at the head of a broad sweep of steps.*

2 *In front of the Capitol at Volubilis stood the Basilica, the law courts, with a podium to give orators height as* *they addressed the crowds before them in the Forum.*

3 *At Leptis Magna the Severan Forum is surrounded by a series of arcades whose arches are decorated at their intersections with remarkably striking, deeply carved and drilled, heads of Medusa.*

BELOW **4** *The theatre at Leptis Magna was a gift to the city by a wealthy citizen, Annobal Tapapius Rufus. A natural slope was utilised in its construction to produce an elegantly curving cavea which enjoyed a magnificent view out to sea over the scaenae frons. Several hundred statues once decorated the building; here on the left is a white marble seated statue of Niobe, the tragic mother whose six sons were slain by the arrows of Apollo and whose six daughters were slain by Diana. The legend tells how, overcome by her misfortune, she was turned to stone.*

OPPOSITE **5** *The magnificent baths at Leptis Magna were built by Hadrian in AD 126-127. They are amongst the largest in the Roman world and covered about half the area of the later Baths of Caracalla in Rome. Still guarding the lofty entrance is a seated figure of Mars. Every bodily comfort was provided in the baths and, for the mind, there was even a library.*

6 *Under Septimius Severus in the late second century* AD *Leptis Magna enjoyed the Imperial favour of her most famous son. The remains of the vast new Forum-Bailica complex he initiated have only been cleared in recent years. At one end of the 300 x 200 metre Forum was a series of shops with elegantly proportioned stone fronts.*

7 *The cold plunge bath in the Hadrianic Baths at Leptis Magna is rectangular, surrounded by columns and pleasant arches. On the edge of the bath is a life-size statue in white marble of Hadrian's young favourite, Antinous, in the guise of Apollo. Antinous was drowned in the Nile in Egypt whilst on a visit there with Hadrian.*

8 *The temple of Jupiter on the Capitol at Sheitla is one of a resplendent trio set side by side and presumed dedicated (in the absence of any inscriptions) to Jupiter, Juno and Minerva. It faces out onto an enclosed court entered through an arch dedicated to Antoninus Pius. Like so many other Capitols in Roman North Africa, it dates to the great period of building in the mid-second century AD.*

9 *The theatre at Sabratha is the most impressive in North Africa and the most substantial of the buildings remaining in the city. Built in the early second century* AD *under the Antonines, it was largely reconstructed by Italian archaeologists for modern performances.*

OPPOSITE ABOVE **10** *The scaenae frons of the theatre at Sabratha has 96 columns in three orders and has been restored to its original height of almost 23 metres. Built in the usual manner of Roman North Africa, facing out to a magnificent sea view, its patrons when seated would have lost this to the imposing stage building.*

OPPOSITE **11** *A low stone apron fronted the stage of the theatre at Sabratha and separated it from the auditorium. Alternate half-round and rectangular niches held 21 reliefs, each reflecting an aspect of the Roman theatre. Each end is decorated with a large sculpture of a three-dimensional dolphin and a panel nearby represents the Three Graces and the Judgement of Paris.*

12 *At Bulla Regia many of the grander villas were built partly underground as a protection from the fierce Numidian heat. The House of the Chase, excavated in 1973, takes its name from a spirited mosaic of huntsmen on foot and horseback found in an upper room. The atrium, below ground and surrounded by a colonnade, also has magnificent mosaics in its side rooms.*

of the proportion and style of the architecture of the much later Georgian period. Similar door frames can also be seen in the market at Perge, though these do not have any carved decoration. Another feature indicative of an Eastern influence is the plain, leafed palmette combined with the acanthus design in the capitals of the columns adjacent to the shop fronts. It is quite likely that some of these features came to Leptis from Syria and Asia Minor under the influence of Julia Domna who, being an intelligent woman and interested in the arts, could well have been conversant with the trends in eastern architecture.

The length of the Basilica was equivalent to the entire width of the Forum and it was built adjacent to the north-east wall. Here there are long white marble pilasters on either side of the apse, carved with the Labours of Hercules and scenes from the life of Dionysus (*Ill. 24, 25*). Both these deities were patrons of the Severan household and the reliefs are deeply carved into the marble. Although they have suffered in part from the centuries of exposure they do not, in spite of being pagan, appear to have been actively defaced when the building was consecrated by the Byzantines.

24, 25 *Under Septimius Severus a great new, three-aisled and 30-metre high basilica was built at Leptis Magna. At each end the white marble pilasters were deeply carved with scenes from the lives of Hercules and Dionysus, the patron deities of both the city and the Imperial family. These details show, left, Hercules strangling the Nemean Lion and, right, Dionysus with his attendant panther in the foliage above him.*

26 *Detail of the elegant balustrade that separates the Nymphaeum from the street at Leptis Magna.*

Apart from the improvements to the water supply and the harbour installations, Severus built the grandiose Nymphaeum which graced the end of a new street of colonnades that led from the harbour to the large palaestra adjacent to the Baths. The low balustrade that separates it from the street was carved in a crossed lattice design, also reminiscent of a design used on a balustrade in the theatre at Perge and again one is reminded of the Georgian period (*Ill. 26*).

To commemorate his visit and to register their appreciation for what he had done to improve his home town, the citizens raised and dedicated to Severus in AD 203 a unique, four-way, Triumphal Arch. This was situated at the southern aspect of the city, spanning the intersection of the main Cardo with the road leading from the West Gate to the Baths. The four friezes at the top of the Arch were scenes in bas relief of cavalry, sacrifices, battles, and the ceremonial entry into Leptis of Severus, pictured riding in a chariot with his two sons, Caracalla and Geta. However Julia, who was with him in Leptis at the time, does not seem to figure in this relief.

Some of these friezes are now badly damaged and they are displayed in the precincts of the Tripoli Museum. Recent work at Aphrodisias in Anatolia, a city not far from Colossae (which was associated with St Paul), has shown that here in the city there was an important school of sculpture, the marble quarries being not too far distant. Their works were well known throughout the Roman world and many fine examples have been found which are now in the Aphrodisias Museum. Some of the artists could well have travelled to Leptis to work *in situ*, for it seems likely that much of the work in Leptis of the Severan period could be attributed to them. Apart from the bas reliefs, the Triumphal Arch was richly decorated with designs crisply cut in the stone (*Ill. 27*) and this, together with the full frontal representation of Severus with his sons in the chariot would seem to be, once again, indicative of a Near Eastern

influence. No traffic was allowed to pass through the Arch, it had to go around, for it was protected by a series of steps and remained an island in the centre of the crossroads. Whilst he was in Africa, Severus made extensive tours to many other cities, some of them being raised to the status of 'Colony'. Numidia, however, which had ranked previously only as a Diocese, he made into an independent Province. Its administration was handed over to the commander of the Third Augustan Legion, who also had to be responsible for the financial control under the supervision of a procurator.

27 The four-way Triumphal Arch built to commemorate Septimius Severus' visit to his native city in AD 203 was magnificently decorated with sculpture and relief. Some elements, such as this fragment of finely carved pediment, still lie near the site.

Sabratha

The ruins of Sabratha lie some forty-five miles west of Tripoli, the Oea of the Emporia, of which nothing remains today but the Triumphal Arch surrounded by the modern city. The ruins are not, in the main, so well preserved as those at Leptis, but it too was a maginificent site overlooking the sea (*Ill. 28*). The coastal road of Nerva went through the town as the Cardo Maximus, most of the civic buildings and the Forum being on the seaward side. The Curia and the Basilica of Justinian were situated on this north or seaward side of the Forum, whilst the temple of Serapis and the Capitolium were built on the west side. This was approached by a flight of steps, the podium still retaining the vestiges of some of the columns. Here too, on the opposite side of the Forum was the large enclosure of the temple to Liber Pater and next to it the Antonine

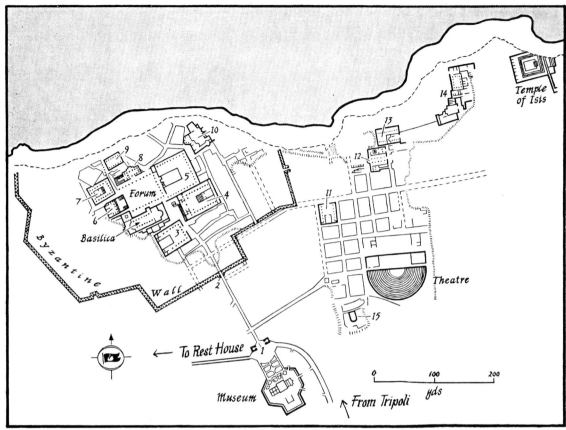

temple. The south side was taken up with the original Basilica, the old law courts, and the south Forum temple, but very little of these structures are still standing today.

Adjacent to the temple of Liber Pater were the Seaward Baths; the interesting feature that still exists here is the sumptuous latrines which were flushed with a constant flow of water (*Ill. 29*). It was a palatial and cool marble hall with the stone seating arranged in an arc against the furthest wall, those seated looking into the expanse of the hall and at a statue set against the opposite wall. The same arrangement was repeated, in a similar palatial style, in the latrines that were set on either side of the swimming pool in the Hadrianic Baths at Leptis. This, which to us in the present day is usually a very private function, was to the Romans a gregarious affair with no inhibitions and must have been accompanied by a great deal of chitchat and bonhomie. These retreats are found throughout the cities of the empire in varying degrees of sophistication. Those at Ephesus next to the palaestra and the adjacent brothel, though not so spacious, were still fitted out in white marble. A unique example, however, is that at Timgad, near the Forum. It is a small dual construction with arms in stone on either side carved in the shape of dolphins – a very cosy arrangement!

The one monument left in Sabratha which gives some indication of

28 *Plan of Sabratha.*
1 Entrance to the excavations;
2 Byzantine Gate; 3 South Forum Temple; 4 Antonine Temple; 5 Temple of Liber Pater; 6 Capitol; 7 Temple of Serapis; 8 Curia; 9 Basilica of Justinian; 10 Seaward Baths; 11 Temple of Hercules; 12, 13 Christian Basilicas; 14 Baths of Oceanus; 15 Peristyle house.

29 *In the Seaward Baths at Sabratha the seating for the public lavatories was arranged around the edges of a spacious marble hall. A feature of them was their mechanics, which allowed a constant flushing with running water.*

how the town appeared to the citizens in the early centuries AD is the theatre (Plate 9). It was also situated close to the sea, built with stone of a much redder tint, and was a good deal larger than the one at Leptis. It had a far more elaborate *scaenae frons*, which was put up between AD 161–69 during the reign of the Emperors Marcus Aurelius and Lucius Verus. It is built as a series of galleries three storeys high (Plate 10), supported by many variegated columns in the red marble which came from the

30 *Detail of one of the 21 panels of relief that decorated the apron of the stage at Sabratha (see Plates 10, 11). This shows the Three Graces and part of another relief to the left, the Judgement of Paris, where Venus is seen presenting an impromptu striptease to influence Paris' decision.*

quarries of Simitthus near Bulla Regia in Tunisia. The auditorium was separated from the stage by a low stone apron, elaborately carved with allegorical figures, amongst them the Three Graces (*Ill. 30*), and the masks of tragedy and humour in the Pompeian style (*Ill. 31*) each end of the apron being decorated with the large figure of a dolphin (Plate 11). Very similar bas reliefs to these masks can be seen in the Villa of the Golden Cupid in Pompeii, which could have belonged to an actor or someone closely connected with the theatre.

The theatre has been well restored and now has an air about it that is a little reminiscent of a palatial music hall. One can well imagine the audience here enjoying those racy productions referred to by Lucius Apuleius. Apuleius was born in Madauros near Carthage in AD 125 and went to Carthage University. He was of Numidian stock from some generations back who, at an early age, was left a considerable fortune by his father. On the strength of this windfall he went to Athens to study Plato and from there went on to Italy. Shortly after reaching Rome, the remainder of his fortune disappeared into the fleshpots and he was obliged to return to North Africa. On his way home he stayed at Oea and, as luck would have it, he met a friend of his from his student days in Carthage who was living with his wealthy widowed mother. Apuleius promptly married her. He was arraigned before the magistrates in the old law courts in the Forum at Sabratha, for it was considered that this

31 *Actors' masks represented in relief on the apron of the stage at Sabratha.*

alliance could only have been brought about by the use of witchcraft. Apuleius, who brilliantly conducted his own defence, was acquitted and returned to Carthage with Amelia Prundentilla, his elderly wife.

Apuleius' *Apologia* which relates to the affair is one of the works to have come down to the present day, together with his masterpiece, *The Golden Ass*. The latter is a light-hearted story, racy, and what could have been the first pornographic novel, worse apparently in the unabridged Latin. It does, however, end on a religious note for he was very interested in the Egyptian cult of Isis. It gives a good insight into the way of life of some sections of the community in those days, again not so far removed from the present.

Apart from the Seaward Baths there were the large Baths of Oceanus to the east of the town, also by the sea, and further east still are the ruins of the temple of Isis. The only other structure of note is the Perystile House which has a fine series of standing columns on its foundations. In the Byzantine period two Christian basilicas were built between the Baths of Oceanus and the theatre. From one of these came the mosaic of the heavenly paradise now in the adjacent museum. The economy of the city, which was also of Punic origin, was dependent upon olives and grain, and possibly fishing, but mainly from the trade derived from the goods brought in by the trans-Saharan caravans.

7

The Military Towns and Roads

The first camp to be established by the Third Augustan Legion when it arrived in North Africa in 30 BC was at Ammaedara (modern Haidra), in the western Aures Mountains. The Legion was made up of some 12,000 men and the garrison remained there a few years until it was moved for strategic reasons to nearby Theveste (Tebessa). During their occupation of Haidra they had to contend with the uprisings of the Garamantes in Libya, an uprising that was put down by the Proconsul, Cornelius Balbus; in AD 17 they also had to deal with the revolt of Tacfarinas. He had once been recruited into the Legion as an auxiliary, but had deserted to lead the tribe of the Musulamii against the Romans.

In AD 14, just before Augustus died, the first military road from Haidra to the Oasis of Gafsa was laid down by the Legion. It passed through the town of Thelepte, which had been built in a desert waste, again very possibly for strategic purposes. All that remain of the town today, however, are the ruins of the baths which in the past could accommodate up to one thousand people. The Romans penetrated beyond Gafsa as far as the Oasis of Nefta, but in Gafsa, an oasis more easily accessible from the coast, they have left as a legacy a large cistern measuring 23 metres long by 5 metres wide and 6 metres deep. It is built with blocks of well-dressed stone with an inscription on the far wall and has a flight of steps going down into the water that rises from a pure clear spring (*Ill. 32*). There are over a hundred or more such springs and cisterns in the oasis, but this particular bath serves as a lido for the nut-brown children diving for coins. Legend has it that Gafsa was founded by Hercules, and throughout its early history it was an important base, which at one time came under the influence of Egyptian rule, before it eventually passed to Carthage. The oasis became a retreat for the Numidian kings when Carthage fell and, during the Jugurthine Wars, the Roman legions, on hearing that Jugurtha had taken refuge there, made a forced march in 106 BC across the desert in an effort to enforce a confrontation.

From Gafsa a road built by Tiberius traversed the ninety miles of flat, arid, and grey brown waste to the Oasis of Gabes, which lies practically

on the coast in the Gulf of the same name (*Ill. 33*). Ten miles out of Gafsa the modern highway follows the ancient road. It skirts the tip of the dried-up salt flats of the Chott Guetta and the Chott Djerid further to the south-east, both of which reflect the shimmering white-hot glare of the sun. These were the legendary Lagoons of the Tritons, so-called for it was here that the ancients asserted that Jason had lost his way with the Argos.

When Julius Caesar was in North Africa fighting his last campaigns of the Civil Wars, Sallust was with him and, in 46 BC, after his final victories, Caesar appointed him to be the Governor of the region. Sallust has recorded in his histories of the wars that, 'Here the hot winds rise like the tempests at sea and the sands fill the face and eyes'. They still do.

Between Garbes and Gafsa there were five resting stages for the legions, who foot slogged the distance in full kit taking with them their water supplies in bullock skins. Even though they often marched at night it was still a far from pleasant journey and not very pleasant today, even with modern transport. At a later date Thelepte became the centre of a

32 *The great Roman cistern at Gafsa with its remarkably preserved and finely laid masonry still maintains its original function, at least for the children of the town.*

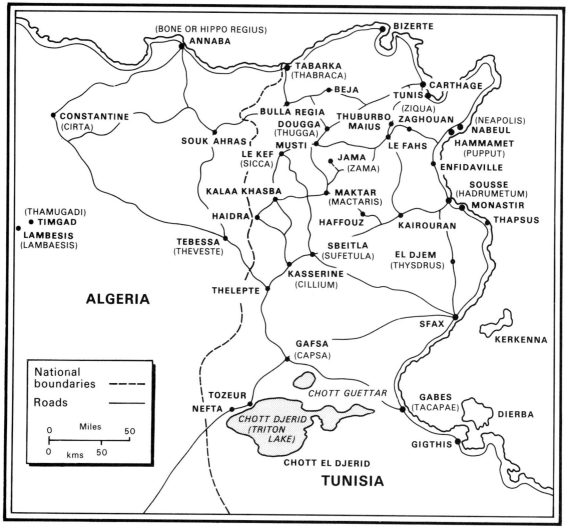

33 *Map of Roman Tunisia.*

road junction between the highway of Hadrian and that which went on to Cilium and the Kasserine Pass, thence on to Sbeitla. Little is left of Cilium now apart from the ruins of its theatre, but nearby is the mausoleum to Flavius Secundus, carved with his obituary, a poem of 110 lines. An inscription was also found in Cilium recording the fact that a veteran who had decided to settle in the district, after leaving the legion, was the first to grow grapes in the area.

Sbeitla, the Suffetula of the Romans further down the road, is noted for its fine series of temples that face the Forum, approached through an arch dedicated to Antoninus Pius. They are ascribed to Jupiter, Juno and Minerva and stand impressively on their podiums reached by flights of steps (Plate 8). It was a town of importance in the first and second centuries, but today it is a somewhat barren site. The Arch of Diocletian, with its splendid proportions, stands isolated in amongst the rubble of the town. There are the vestigial remains of the baths and the amphitheatre, but more is left of the theatre itself, placed in an idyllic situation beside the river. Both Romans and Greeks had an instinct for town planning, be it in Asia Minor or wherever, and they unerringly picked the most suitable sites for their public buildings. The theatres are nearly always built into the side of a hill, with the audience looking onto the *scaenae frons*, beyond which there was, as often as not, a natural scenic back-drop.

In the rubble between the Arch and the baths are the remains of a private plunge bath decorated with marine mosaics, which at one time must have belonged to a wealthy private villa (*Ill. 34*). Cultivation of the olive was the basis of the local economy and here in the town there are the remains of several large oil presses (*Ill. 35*). During the first and second centuries the Legion found that the town, and the surrounding district, could be relied upon for a steady source of recruits.

In the Christian period Sbeitla became a Bishopric with three principal churches, that of St Vitalis still having in the the ruins of its baptistry an unusual font (*Ill. 36*). It is cruciform, with steps leading down into it and

34 *A wall mosaic with an attractive group of various fishes decorates the apsidal end of a small private bath in a rich villa at Sbeitla.*

out, indicative to those who were being baptised that they were leaving the old life behind and ascending into a new. It is covered in mosaic and bears the Saint's name, the sides resembling a large cushion. Immediately adjacent to it is the Church of Bellator, having a similar font but not so lavishly decorated, and a small temple not far from the theatre was taken and converted into the Chapel of Servius by the Donatists.

To deal with any tribal uprisings, and to reach any trouble spot as quickly as possible before a situation could develop into something more serious, the Legion moved in AD 75 a little further west of Haidra to Theveste (Tebessa), which was still in the Aures Mountains, and left their veterans behind at Haidra to farm the country. Today Haidra is an exposed and windswept site, but it does have left standing an important mausoleum, one of three, which is typical of the period. There is also an arch to Septimius Severus spanning what was once the Decumanus Maximus. There are also the scanty remains of the theatre, a large military cemetery relating to the Legion, and the ruins of several churches.

After the Legion had established its new headquarters in Tebessa, the town was developed on the grid principle of Hippodamus, but this has almost been obliterated by the modern town. The few monuments left are the Arch of Caracalla in the later town walls, the temple of Minerva

35 *Olive production was a staple of Sheitla and, as well as the large commercial factories, there were a number of smaller installations such as this example with its circular mill or grinding platform and a small trough in the foreground to receive the oil.*

which stands on a podium four metres high and houses the museum and, lastly, the ruins of the amphitheatre. The doors to the rooms where the gladiators used to wait and where the wild beasts were kept before taking part in the spectacles are still there intact. In some gardens not far from the Arch of Caracalla stands what at one time was the largest basilica to be built in North Africa. Dedicated to St Crispin it is remarkable for its fine stone ornamentation. Nearby, and situated on a lower level, are the catacombs that were used for the early Christian burials.

In AD 73 Vespasian built a road from Tebessa to the port of Hippo Regius, which had been enlarged to take the supplies for the town and the Third Augustan Legion; at a later date another road was laid down from Tebessa to Carthage. A further road, built by Trajan, went south across the mountains to the Gulf of Syrte, which was then linked up with a series of forts for protection. The roads commonly followed the ancient Punic dirt tracks, but most were entirely new projects. They were laid out in excavated tracks several feet wide, the base was filled with a hard core of consolidated stones and finally infilled with a topping of smaller stones; the surface finally cambered for drainage. Wherever possible valleys were avoided and the roads kept to the higher ground in as straight a line as the terrain would allow. Sharp bends in the road were difficult for the Roman waggons to negotiate, owing to the fact that they all had fixed

36 The mosaic encrusted baptismal font in the Basilica of St Vitalis at Sbeitla carries the Saint's name on its edge. The steps at either end allowed for the total immersion of the candidate and there is a Chi-Rho monogram set in the mosaic base between the steps.

axles. When there was no option but to pass through a valley the road was protected with more towers and military look-outs built on the higher ground.

This network of roads which increasingly spread out from Tebessa and Carthage amounted in the end to an aggregate of more than 12,000 miles; many were marked with milestones dedicated to those emperors who had been involved with their construction. As they developed so more and more towns sprang up alongside, often only a few miles apart; over the years at least 300 towns were founded in Algeria and Tunisia alone. Many of these are now just ground plans and lost in a heap of stones, whilst those that developed on the sites of old Punic towns are better preserved.

Hadrian moved the camp of the legion yet again in AD 128. This time to Lambaesis, still in the Aures Mountains, where it remained permanently for the next three hundred years to become the Aldershot of North Africa. Once more it was for strategic reasons in order to gain even greater control over the nomadic tribes. It had a vast area to protect with a relatively small number of troops; in this they were helped by those

37 *At the springs of Jebel Zaghouan Hadrian built a nymphaeum with twelve arched recesses that once held statues. From here water was conducted by aqueduct to Carthage, as it is still by modern pipelines to Tunis.*

veterans who had settled on the outlying frontiers with the desert. In times of acute stress reinforcements were sent to Africa, usually from the legions in Spain and Gaul. An inscription inscribed on a rock face in the Tighanimine Gorge in the Aures commemorates the building of a road from Lambaesis to Biskra in AD 145 by the Sixth Ferrata Legion. It had been drafted in from Syria to help the Third Augustan consolidate the desert frontiers.

The legions had in their organisation not only the equivalent of the infantry man, but also a full complement of skilled engineers and surveyors – such as the REME of the British Army. Their architects and surveyors not only superintended the building of the camps and towns, but also built the bridges and laid out the roads. They constructed the aqueducts to distribute the water supplies to those cities needing it, where it was stored in large cisterns. They were also responsible for the efficient drainage systems beneath the streets of the towns, which could be reached by a series of stone manhole covers. Building the aqueducts was a highly skilled operation, for in North Africa they could extend many miles. They had to be arranged so that the water flow was even and gradual throughout the entire length; they also had to ensure the correct pressure at the receiving end at the cisterns. An outstanding example of such an aqueduct was that built to take the water from a nymphaeum in the Jebel Zaghouan (*Ill. 37*) to the cisterns at La Malga in Carthage. Built by Hadrian, it collected the water from the springs of the Jebel into a large basin, whence it was fed into the aqueduct which then ran across country some fifty-odd miles (*Ill. 38*). Where hills obstructed the way the

38 *Large upstanding sections of the Roman aqueduct that conveyed water from the springs at Jebel Zaghouan to Carthage still dominate areas of the Tunisian landscape.*

water was taken in conduits driven through them by the engineers. Long sections of the aqueduct are still to be seen stretching across the countryside on the way to Tunis, a tribute to the expertise of those engineers. The springs of the Jebel Zaghouan supply the water for the city of Tunis today and a large new pipeline takes it through those same conduits in the hills which were originally excavated by the legion. The Pioneer Corps of the British Army also had its counterpart in the legion, for they often carried out the work themselves, though much was done with forced labour, or put out to contract. The fact that work was put out to contract has been confirmed in the inscription of Gaius Balbus, who was the Proconsul in Leptis at the time of Augustus, for in it he states that he had auctioned the contracts for the paving of the city.

There was, however, one embarrassing situation that arose in AD 113, and this too has been recorded. A retired surveyor from the Third Augustan, Nonius Datus, had completed the original survey for an aqueduct at Saldae, modern Bejaia. Things had not gone according to plan with the work as it progressed, and he was asked by the procurator of the province, Varius Clemens, for his considered opinion. He states that he met the procurator and that they went to the site, where he found that the digging had strayed from the line. In his report he says, 'The upper tunnel turned right to the south, and likewise the lower tunnel turned north to its right'. In other words, they had missed each other in the mountain. He then states that he set up a competition between the marines and the auxiliary troops so that they linked up and the mountain was pierced. When the water flowed, Varius Clemens, the procurator, dedicated the work. The tunnel was 428 metres long.

In the camp at Lambaesis the Legion was very much a self-contained unit and, as the years went by, life for the men became more comfortable. They had clubs known as Sculoae for their different leisure interests and, no doubt, the centurions had the equivalent of the Sergeants' Mess. They had an amphitheatre too which was very popular; but they were not allowed to marry, an edict abolished by Septimius Severus when he became Emperor, though many entered into common-law liaisons with the local girls. When they became veterans they usually made the contract legal, and then settled near the frontiers on farms, or in the veteran towns. Between the Wars, no soldier in the British army was allowed to marry until he had reached the age of thirty, when he could be 'taken on the strength'; in other words was entitled to a family allowance, living quarters and daily rations such as meat and bread baked in the army bakeries. Today, many British army personnel live near the garrison towns and have their own social clubs. There are – or indeed were – many similarities with the Roman system.

Before he died Caracalla had improved the efficiency of the legion by taking the command out of the hands of the Proconsul, who was elected on a yearly basis, and putting it into the hands of a Legate who had to have a successful military record before he was appointed. As the years went by, many local Africans became more Romanised, spoke the language, and were recruited either into the legion, or into the ancillary units. One such was Lucius Quietus, a Berber from Mauretania, who rose to equestrian rank under the Emperor Domitian and became a cavalry commander. He later served in Dacia and on the Danube under Trajan. He is pictured with his cavalry on Trajan's Column in Rome. His achievements merited a Triumph and he was later made Governor of Mauretania. He then went to Asia and, after a further Triumph awarded for his victories there, he was given the prestigious post of Governor in Palestine. Unfortunately his career came to a sad end when Trajan died, for he fell foul of Hadrian who succeeded him. His troops were disarmed and in protest they rioted, which made a delicate situation much worse and he was executed. Romans of distinction and great ability could often fall from illustrious heights at the drop of a hat.

Several other Africans had notable military careers, one of them becoming the Governor of Mauretania. There was also Lollius Urbicus who was born in the small town of Tiddis, which at that time had a population of only 9000 and was not far from Cirta. His statue used to stand in the Forum at Tiddis and he was its most distinguished son. It has long since disappeared but the base remains and is inscribed, 'To Quintus Lollius Urbicus, son of Marcus, of the tribe Quirina, Legate of Augustus for the province of Lower Germany, priest, Legate of the Emperor Hadrian in the campaign in Judea, in which he was given the special honour of the Golden Crown, Legate of the Tenth Legion Gemina, praetor as Caesar's candidate, Tribune of the Plebs, Legate of the Proconsul of Asia, Tribune with the broad stripe, [this was pre-Senatorial status] of the Twenty-second Legion, member of the Commission of Four for the maintenance of roads, patron of Tiddis, by decree of the Town Councellors – at public expense'. It was some career; he finally became the Governor of Britain to organise the campaign against the Scots and he was then responsible for establishing the frontier, the Antonine Wall, which ran from the Clyde to the Forth. The family tomb is still on the hillside slightly north of Tiddis where the rest of the family are buried, and here they once worked their estates and lived the lives of landed gentry.

Lambaesis

The headquarter camp at Lambaesis was built by the Third Augustan to a rectangular plan and with military precision, the buildings being bisected by two main streets, the Via Principalis, and the Via Decumana. Both were well paved, with a large four-way arch in two storeys some 30 metres high at the intersection. It had a double series of columns and pillars with rounded niches and a winged Victory decorated the keystone of the central vault. The imposing walls of the Praetorian Hall, which some authorities consider to be the remains of the barracks, are still there. It was a paved courtyard surrounded by porticoes on three sides with rooms opening off them. The Basilica was on the fourth side, 52 × 30 metres. There were temples to Mars and Minerva, and the Genius of the Camp, together with the rooms of the military guilds and the quarters of the Commander-in-Chief. The amphitheatre is located to the east of the

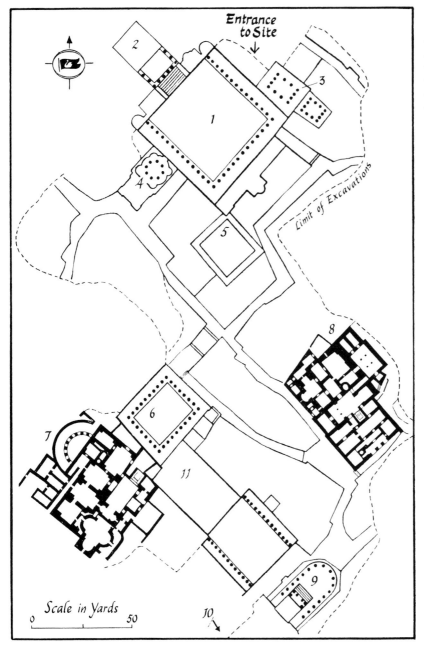

39 *Plan of Thuburbo Maius.*
1 Forum; 2 Capitol; 3 Curia;
4 Temple of Mercury;
5 Market; 6 Portico of the
Petronii; 7 Summer Baths;
8 Winter Baths; 9 Temple of
Baal; 10 To the amphitheatre;
11 Church.

Hall and, though badly ruined, it still has the remains of the underground passages and the rooms where the beasts were kept. Little remains of the nearby garrison town which was occupied by some of the veterans and their families, but it also had all the facilities of a town of the period which included shops, temples, a Capitol and a theatre.

Severus visited the camp some time after his arrival in Africa in AD 202 and he had the Via Principalis paved with white limestone. To commemorate this visit the usual practice of raising a Triumphal Arch was followed; it still stands between the town and the camp.

Thuburbo Maius

The veterans towns and colonies were set up to accommodate those who had had long service with the legions; they came not only from the Third Augustan at Lambaesis but also from other legions serving throughout the Empire. The land awarded to the veterans often amounted to as much as three-quarters of an acre, allowing them to settle themselves and their families. The colonies they founded were also a part of a strategic plan, enabling Rome to use their expertise and training to help look after those frontiers which were not so easily defended. Some were established in the hills but in parts of Numidia where the country was much flatter and gave on to the desert, a system of *fossae* or ditches called the *limes* were dug and extended in depth for as much as twenty miles. The area here was inhabited mainly by farmers, often with fortified farms, but it was also guarded by a series of towers and fortresses put up and maintained by detachments of the Third Augustan Legion. It was part of a line of defence against tribal hostility. Echoes of the system are still apparent in the fortified Berber towns in the Ziz valley and beyond the Atlas in Morocco.

One of the early veteran colonies was at Thuburbo Maius, a very short way from Fahs, which itself was also a very minor Roman settlement. Thuburbo was originally of Berber origin and was later taken over and developed into a Punic town. After the conquest of Eygpt, Augustus decided in 27 BC to settle a large number of his veterans here and in Hadrian's time it became known as the Colonia Julia Aurelia Commoda. It was a muddle of a city with narrow alleys and no town planning, but it did have some fine villas and outstanding civic buildings (*Ill. 39*). The remains of the Capitol (*Ill. 40*), built on a podium, and reached by a broad flight of steps, still has some columns standing. It stood in a Forum some 43 metres square, dominating the whole area, but it is sad that the stone paving has long since disappeared. It was dedicated to Jupiter Capitolinus and, beneath the feet of the huge statue of the god which stood in the cella, are the rooms that once housed the town's archives and the other municipal paraphenalia.

The small temple of Mercury, which must have been a little architectural gem, looks on to the Forum from the right-hand aspect and the ruins of a small square market are to be found behind the south-east corner. A central wall remains standing and there are two porticos that give on to shops with their various mosaic floors. Many other mosaic floors with complicated geometric designs are still *in situ*, and in most cases these are well preserved (*Ill. 41*). There were two municipal baths, the Winter and the Summer establishments, the latter being the larger of the two and covering 2800 square metres. In the past the walls had a marble facing and here, too, there are more fine mosaic floors. The Winter Baths were entered through a large portico from the Street of the

40 *The Capitol at Thuburbo Maius, with its nine-metre high columns, dominates the north-west side of the Forum.*

41 *A feature on the site at Thuburbo Maius is the number of complicated geometric design mosaics that can still be seen* in situ.

Waggoner, the complex having twenty rooms, one of them being a large hall with benches around the walls to recline on. Here again there are fine floors and a ceiling that was supported by beautifully marked, red marble columns, from the quarries at Simitthus.

There were some large mansions near the civic centre, the most important being the House of the Labyrinth which occupied an area equivalent to a whole block, and the House of the Waggoner a little further away. Some way out of the civic centre and at the end of the Street of the Waggoner, there is a small temple to Baal that rises up from a podium which is enclosed by a small walled precinct and gives on to another small Forum surrounded by porticos. The temple is an example of the aptitude the Romans had, after a passage of time, for assimilating the cults of those they had conquered into their own pantheon of deities. On the hill just beyond the temple to Baal are the remains of the Christian Basilica, an extensive site, with a cruciform font sunk into what was once the floor of the baptistry (*Ill. 42*). It is the Corinthian Portico supported on black marble columns that is, however, the outstanding monument (Ill. 43). Adjacent to the Portico were rooms that opened out on to it, and on to the palaestra. In one of these with a marble floor there was a shrine

42 *Ruins of the extensive Christian Basilica at Thuburbo Maius with a sunken font in the foreground.*

dedicated to Aesculapius, the god of healing. The animated mosaic of boxers that can be seen in the Bardo was found here and it was this mosaic that identified the area as being a palaestra. An inscription records that the portico was built and presented to the town by Petronius Felix and his sons in AD 225 and it is situated at the end of the street of the Petronii, not far from the Summer Baths.

In spite of the fine civic buildings and the villas, the town did not develop over the years to any great extent and, for the most part, remained rather provincial. In September the countryside is covered with a big, plantain-like plant, bearing large, light mauve, bell-shaped flowers which form a cushion of colour on the flat green leaves. One cannot help but wonder if the forebears of these plants were flowering in the countryside, around the town, in the first and second centuries.

43 The magnificent Corinthian Portico of the Petronii at Thuburbo Maius was given to the town by Petronius Felix and his sons in AD 225. It forms part of the palaestra, a gymnasium.

Djemila

Djemila and Timgad in Algeria were the two most important towns that were founded and built solely for the veterans with the aid of the Third Augustan. Djemila, meaning 'The Beautiful', was given this name by the Arabs, but it was known to the Romans as Cuicul. It was founded by Nerva for his veterans and was situated on a spur between two valleys, the site being quite remarkable for the wide ranging views over the surrounding hilly landscapes. The town appears to flow gently down the hillside like the icing on a long sugar bun. The ruins are in an unusual state of preservation, for one can walk down the streets to the Forum and markets which, with little stretch of the imagination, can live again.

The lower part of the town was the original settlement and had a degree of town planning, but this was lost to a certain extent as it spread up the hill during the first and second centuries. This was largely due to the influx of merchants, local tradespeople and labourers who depended on the town for a living. Some of the important families connected with Djemila are referred to in inscriptions that date from the Severan period. Tiberius Claudius Subadus was one who rose to great eminence in the Empire becoming a Senator and, from AD 208–210, the Governor of Numidia. His brother, Claudius Aquila, did almost as well for he became a member of the equestrian nobility and a Prefect of Egypt.

The Cardo Maximus traverses the length of the oldest part of Djemila from east to west, most of the buildings lying west of the street (Plate 17; *Ill. 44*). Here one finds the North Forum, bordered by porticos and shops, which was built at the end of the first century and covered an area

44 *From the Cardo Maximus, the main street of Djemila, there is a maginificent view out over the surrounding countryside, underlining the care with which the Roman surveyors selected their town sites and laid them out.*

of 48 × 44 metres. On the north side another portico of six columns of the Corinthian order gives on to the Capitol, and near by is the small Curia. The Capitol was dedicated to Jupiter, Juno and Minerva, the patrons of Djemila. A small enclosed, almost square, market which backed on to a wall of the Capitol, was built by the two brothers Lucius and Caius Cosinius (Plate 16). It was entered from the Cardo Maximus and had a central pool with eighteen shops around the walls. Here in the pondericum were kept the official tables of weights and measures, and a stone table with three cavities carved into it, each differing in size, was used as the official standard of measure for volume. This is still *in situ* and gives an uncanny impression of recent use (*Ill. 45*). There is an intimate feeling about the market in general and the inscription on the portico records that the brothers donated it to the town at a cost of 30,000 sestertii.

The Capitol Baths were near the Forum, and beyond this complex are the ruins of a large mansion, the House of Europa, so-called from its fine mosaic floor depicting the Rape of Europa by Jupiter. The other baths in the old part of the town were those of Longinianus and Terentius, two other wealthy citizens who built them at their own expense. Other fine villas in the town were those of Castorius, Amphitrite, and Bacchus, all of them having fine mosaics. There are also the remains of a residential district which was not quite so salubrious.

The new town developed from the time of Septimius Severus onward, centred around the paved expanse of a large Forum. It is dominated by Severus' majestic temple, which was reached by one of the most impressive flights of steps ever to be built to such an edifice in North Africa (*Ill. 46*). It is another example of the Roman ability to use a site to the best possible advantage. It was completed after Severus' death in AD 229 and the columns, many of them still standing, were 8.4 metres high. A very fine portrait of Severus in marble came from this temple. It

13 *Marble portrait head of Septimius Severus from the Temple of the Severi at Djemila. The curled locks of his beard are a particular feature of his portraits* *later in his reign and have close affinities with representations of the Egyptian god Serapis.*

OPPOSITE ABOVE **14** *The location of the Arch of Caracalla at Djemila emphasises the starkness of the countryside surrounding this veterans colonia, built between two wadis on a ridge 900 metres above sea level.*

OPPOSITE **15** *The Arch of Caracalla at Djemila stands at the east end of one of the two fora that the town possessed. In AD 216 Caracalla took the unprecedented step of granting citizenship to all the peoples of the Roman provinces; hitherto it was only acquired as a birthright or by various means, such as having served 25 years in the legions. The Arch marks the gratitude of the inhabitants of Djemila towards the Emperor for the grant.*

ABOVE **16** *The small market of Cosinus at Djemila had 18 shops and a good situation close to the Capitol. Cosinus was a Carthaginian merchant who donated the market to the town, and it is recorded that it cost him 18,000 sesterces.*

17 *A public fountain in the main street, the Cardo Maximus, of Djemila illustrates the typical civic pride of so many of the North African towns.*

18 *The magnificent Arch of Trajan at Timgad with its triple-opening is more correctly called the Lambaesis Gate. It dominates the site, the 'Algerian Pompeii', and stands at the centre of a neatly laid out network of roads and monuments, founded under Trajan in* AD *100 as a properly grid-planned veterans colonia.*

19 *Typical of so many of the fine streets in the Roman cities of North Africa this example at Timgad is still well paved, lined with columns and leads to an imposing arch whilst beyond, the rolling countryside stretches away.*

20 *The Capitol at Dougga stands high above the town which itself is 700 metres above sea level. It was built* *in* AD *166-167 under Marcus Aurelius and is one of the most imposing monuments of Roman North Africa.*

21 *For all the size of Dougga and its many temples, it is rather curious that its theatre was relatively small; its seating capacity was around 3,500. Following Vitruvian precepts, the acoustics were much improved by incorporating earthenware pots in the upper walls.*

OPPOSITE ABOVE **22** *The inscription on the Arch of Trajan that dominates the Forum at Maktar records that it and the Forum were built in AD 116. It has a commanding position on the highest point of the town.*

OPPOSITE **23** *The palaestra was an essential part of the Schola of the Juvenes at Maktar where the paramilitary group of youthful members of Romanised Punic families could take its exercise.*

24 *The amphitheatre at El Djem is the sixth largest in the Roman world, but it seems even larger as it rises out of the flat landscape and high above the single-storey Arab houses that cluster around it.*

25 *As with most amphitheatres in the Roman world, that at El Djem had extensive passageways and rooms beneath the central oval where victims, animal as well as human, would be kept until they were called upon to appear for the entertainment of the howling mob.*

is now in the local museum and has all the hallmarks of being a convincing and accurate likeness (Plate 13).

At the opposite end of the Forum is the Arch of Caracalla (Plate 14), put up by the citizens in AD 216 to commemorate the granting of citizenship to all the peoples of the Roman provinces; this too is monumental and majestic (Plate 15). It dominates the east end of the Forum and balances the Temple of Severus at the further corner. Behind the Arch is the cloth market, built by Rutilius Saturninus in AD 367, and behind this structure one finds the public latrines, which are definitely not so luxurious as those of Leptis or Thuburbo Maius.

The South Baths were built in the new part of the town in AD 183 by the Emperor Commodus and they covered 2600 square metres. These too are in a good state of preservation and they have a paved terrace which looks out over the town. In the frigidarium is a cold plunge which has the unusual measurement of 13 metres in length. To the west of the Severan Forum is the theatre, and here again it is situated to take advantage of the extensive views over the surrounding hills (*Ill. 47*). It is

46 *The temple of Severus at Djemila is set at the end of the Forum which he built, and is approached by a magnificent flight of steps. A splendid portrait bust of the emperor was found here in the temple (see Plate 13). From it there are extensive views over the surrounding countryside.*

also in good condition, having two tiers of seats that could accommodate 3000 people if necessary, and a stage with some elaborate decoration.

In the fifth century during the Christian period, Djemila spread even further up the hill and became a Bishopric under Bishop Cresconius. Two basilicas were built around this time, the larger having five aisles and some mosaic floors that were donated by the parishioners. Numerous artefacts from the area are in the museum, including amongst other things, bronzes, collections of jewellery and the many other accoutrements which were a part of life in those days; they testify to the considerable wealth that many of the citizens enjoyed over the years.

47 *Like most of the theatres in Roman North Africa, the theatre at Djemila makes use of a hollow in the hillside for its auditorium and enjoys breathtaking views out beyond the* scaenae frons, *here over countryside instead of a seascape as at Leptis Magna and Sabratha.*

Timgad

Timgad was known to the Romans as Thamugaddi. It was entirely different from Cuicul in concept and its surroundings, being situated not in the hills, but in flat country lying at the foot of the Aures Mountains. It was in an area that was policed from early on by the Third Augustan Legion with a series of military camps, put there to keep watch on the unruly Berber tribes who lived in their villages in the mountains and foothills.

Timgad was founded by Trajan in AD 101 as the Colonia Marciana Traiana Thamugaddi, possibly on an old Berber settlement judging from the name. Amongst the veterans who settled there were some who had served in the Legio Ulpa Victrix during the Parthian Wars. It began its development under the direction of Munatus Gallus, Trajan's Legate at the time, and it was laid out with military precision. Each side was 350 metres long and the town was divided for the most part into a series of 120 square blocks, or *insulae*, with intersecting streets. The Decumanus Maximus (Plate 19) bisected the town and it stretched from the Mascula Gate, built by Marcus Aurelius, to the splendid Lambaesis Gate, also known as Trajan's Arch (Plate 18), the street then leading on to the old road to Lambaesis, which was not so far distant.

The Cardo Maximus entered the town by the Cirta or North Gate, which halved this part of the city into equal blocks of thirty-two insulae, occupied mostly by private buildings and shops, and then led to steps which gave on to a paved and spacious Forum (*Ill. 48*). Beyond the Forum, built into the side of the only small hill on the site, is the theatre which could seat up to 5000 people and from the topmost rows of seats one can look out over the *scaenae frons* to an extensive view of the whole town. From here one can see the expanse of Forum with the Basilica on the east side, to the large podium used by the orators near the Curia on the

48 *Timgad in Algeria is the best preserved and neatly laid out city of Roman North Africa. Planned by Trajan on a regular grid of 1200 Roman feet as a colonia for veterans, it is a surveyor's delight with its flat aspect against the spectacular hill locations such as Djemila or Dougga. In this view the site is dominated by the magnificent Arch of Trajan beyond the Forum.*

west. The podium was always put in such a position that the Orator had his back to the prevailing breeze, to enable his voice to carry across to his listeners. The Forum was surrounded by the usual porticoes and, apart from the Basilica and the Curia, it had a small temple to Fortune. Oddly enough there was no Capitol, for this was built outside the original precincts of the town. On the steps to the Forum a citizen, full of the joy of life, has inscribed his personal graffiti. To the east of the forum can be seen the remains of a luxurious villa with a courtyard and a central well; around the court there are several jardinieres decorated with stage masks. Did the occupant by any chance have a connection with the theatre? Was he an actor, an impresario, or was he just what the Spanish would call an officianado? One is reminded of the Villa of the Golden Cupid at Pompeii, decorated with theatrical memorabilia and probably belonging to someone connected with the stage.

Adjacent are the central latrines that have already been mentioned, unusual in the fact that there are two seats together, separated from the other pairs by arm rests carved in the shape of dolphins. The most interesting structure, however, is the library, which an inscription states cost the donor who gave it to the town 400,000 sestertii. It occupies the fifth block off the Cardo Maximus before the street reaches the Forum. It had a handsome semi-circular window in the reading room looking out on to a porticoed court, and in the room there were the recesses for the scrolls and books. It is on one of the columns of this portico that the other graffiti of an unacademic nature are engraved. In the insulae opposite the library there were some shops, and here too were the wealthy villas that belonged to Confidius Crementius and Julius Jannerius.

Timgad had many baths, fourteen separate establishments in all, some minor, but the largest were the Northern and the Southern Baths, the former outside the Cirta Gate, and the latter at the far end of the town. The largest establishment inside the precincts of the old town was the Eastern Baths, near the Decumanus Maximus and not far from the Mascula Gate. There were three markets, the oldest being the eastern market, which was not far from Trajan's Arch and within the town walls. This had an apse with shops and market stalls and was built on two levels. Outside the town walls and not far from the Capitol were the other two, one an old clothes market and the other a much larger structure, was built early in the third century by Sertius (*Ill. 49*). This had a courtyard measuring 38 × 25 metres surrounded by porticos with an apse at the southern end. Sertius was another wealthy citizen of Timgad who lived with his wife in a mansion on the southern perimeter not far from the Capitol; her dignified statue can be seen in the museum. He too built the market at his own expense and donated it to the town, but he did not leave any record as to the cost.

Timgad could also boast of a very efficient drainage system, which went under the Cardo Maximus. It was reached, as at Dougga, by large round, well-fitting manhole covers in heavy paving stone. The system appears to be in good working order even now, which is more that can be said for a modern local system, which seems to be permanently blocked.

During the Christian period the town developed beyond the Capitol, also further to the west, and here was built the Donatist Cathedral. It was the finest in North Africa, 100 metres long, and next to it was the Palace of Bishop Optatus. Timgad had suffered little up to this time from municipal and tribal disturbances. However, after the persecutions of Diocletian, it became involved in the fight between the Donatists and the Catholics for supremacy and Optatus turned the town into a stronghold of the Donatist heresy. Most of those in the surrounding settlements and the mountain villages supported the doctrine and it was at this time that Optatus became one of the fervent leaders of the schism. He was fanatical and had a private army of circumcellonies who were nothing more than a rabble armed with swords and staves. They moved about intimidating and terrorising the countryside with their violence, endeavouring to enforce the Donatist convictions on those Catholics who had not conformed, though they themselves often used the movement more for political than religious reasons. Optatus was strongly supported by Gildo, a member of the Jubaleni tribe of Berbers that had absorbed much of the Roman way of life. He was one of three brothers, the other two

49 *The main market building at Timgad was given to the town by a citizen, Sertius, during the Severan period. It lies just behind the Capitol and Sertius' own house has been identified in the south-west quarter of the town.*

being Firmus and Mascezel the youngest. They had remained loyal to Rome until Firmus, who was the leader of the tribe together with Mascezel, revolted in AD 371–4 and captured Iol Caesarea. Gildo remained loyal whilst Rome defeated Firmus, who then committed suicide, and for this help Gildo was made Count of Africa. Over the years the tribe became very powerful and wealthy, but then Gildo fell foul of Rome and in AD 397 he held up the grain shipments to Ostia. Mascezel by now had made his peace with Rome and was with the force that was sent to subdue Gildo, whose support faded as soon as they landed and he too died shortly after. Optatus was then executed for being involved with Gildo from the outset. His death, however, was not the end of the Donatists in Numidia, for it was still a force until AD 420 when Dulcitius was sent to Numidia by Rome to end the schism. Gaudentius was Bishop at the time and he gathered all the Donatists into the cathedral compound of five acres and threatened to burn it down around their heads. St Augustine's comment was: 'They cannot have the death of Martyrs for they do not have the life of Christians, it would be better for them to perish in their own fires than in the fires of hell doing penance for their dissensions'. Their final fate has not been recorded.

Timgad was eventually taken over by the Byzantines but, after the attentions of the Vandals, it fell into oblivion, to be eventually rediscovered by the Scots traveller James Bruce, who was travelling in the region in 1765.

8

Roman Carthage and the Agricultural Towns

Julius Caesar had had the refounding of Carthage in mind before he died. At a later date Caius Gracchus, too, had advocated the project but, in spite of the fact that a few emigrated from Italy on his recommendation, it was not in the end a successful venture and it was left to Augustus in 29 BC to commence the rebuilding. He raised the status of Carthage to that of Colonnae and transferred 30,000 settlers from Italy to be the first colonists. Under the later emperors it once more became a great city, equally as large as Antioch or Alexandria (*Ill. 50*).

The harbours had to be enlarged to cope with the increasing shipments of grain to Rome and many merchants accumulated great wealth out of the shipping. The mosaic floors in the villas of the rich often had marine motifs which are unique to North Africa (*Ill. 51*), and it is thought that these might reflect their owners' maritime interests. On the side of the hill behind the Antonine Baths can be seen the ruins of what used to be one of these select residential districts. A well paved avenue with fine houses and villas, plinths for statues, wellheads and many other sculptural remains testify to their erstwhile elegance.

The massive baths, which in their day were one of the glories of Carthage, were begun by Hadrian and completed in AD 146 by Antoninus Pius (*Ill. 52*); when finished they rivalled those that Caracalla later built in Rome. They could, in fact, be counted as one of the largest and most sumptuous to be found in the Empire. They were built by the shore and today one can wander around the substantial walls of the basement which once supported the complex of warm rooms and hot rooms and those set aside for resting. Here in the basement were the furnaces and the fuel stores, and here too one can see what remains of the original terracotta pipe plumbing.

A broad staircase led to the baths on the upper floor, which were segregated for the sexes. Here again one must use one's imagination to people this huge structure with the shades of those inhabitants of Carthage who came here to spend their leisure hours gossiping, discussing politics and, without doubt, the various local scandals; or, if

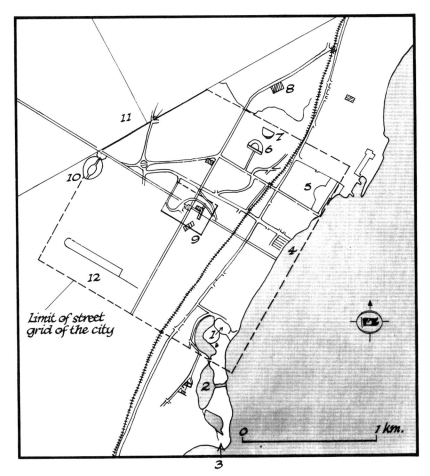

Plan of Carthage. 1 Punic naval harbour; 2 Punic commercial harbour; 3 Entrance to ancient harbours; 4 Late Punic and Roman houses; 5 Antonine Baths and Archaeological Park; 6 Theatre; 7 Odeon; 8 Damoos el Karita; 9 Hill of Byrsa; 10 Amphitheatre; 11 La Malga cisterus; 12 Circus

51 *A remarkable local feature of many of the villas of Roman North Africa is the representation of the myriad marine life off the coasts. This example is from Carthage.*

they were more energetic, exercising in the open palaestras. The ceiling of the frigidarium, which was a vast oblong hall, was supported on four massive granite columns with Corinthian capitals. One can get some idea of the size of this hall when it is realised that each of them was some two metres high and weighed four tons. One of them crashed through the ruins in the distant past to the basement, and here it remained for centuries until it was taken to the centre of a roundabout at a nearby crossroads where, even though floodlit at night, it seems to be out of place and out of context. Nearby are the remains of houses of wealthy Roman owners that were heavily decorated with mosaics and carvings (*Ills. 53, 54*).

There were two theatres. The large one built by Hadrian in AD 125 is said to have had the equivalent of a residential repertory company; it has now been restored and is used for festivals. Apuleius, who has already been mentioned in connection with Sabratha and his novel *The Golden Ass*, once gave a speech here before the production of his *Florides*. It is worth repeating: 'In an auditorium like this, what is important is not the marble pavement, the architecture of the proscenium or the stage

52 The Antonine Baths that lie on the shore and partly submerged today at Carthage are enormous, amongst the largest in the empire. It is difficult to realise when looking at the ruins that the huge chunks of masonry are actually only the remains of the basement structure. An idea of what their superstructure looked like can be obtained from representations on some large, rare Roman lamps.

colonnade; it is not the roof raised on high, the brightly coloured box seats, or the other seats in a semi-circle; it is not the fact that at other times we saw a mime playing his comic roles, a comedian acting, a tragedian reciting, a tight-rope walker risking his life, or a play actor gesticulating, in other words, all kinds of performers present themselves to the public, each according to his art'. How little has changed over the centuries! The Allied Forces assembled here amongst the ruins at the end of the Desert War to be congratulated on their victories by Sir Winston Churchill.

The odeon nearby was a much smaller building complete with orchestra and stage but in this case it did have a roof. Very elegantly decorated with the statues and inscriptions that have been found in its ruins, it originally stood in a courtyard with a portico that was approached from a street liberally scored with the marks of childrens' games. Just after its completion it was used to stage the Pythian Games, but was later on used for concerts and more intimate productions. Regrettably it did not survive the attentions of the Vandals, so hardly anything is left of the original structure.

The amenities of Carthage included a large circus for chariot racing which was on the outskirts of the city next to the amphitheatre. It was a very popular institution with the Carthaginians and the contests usually took place between four teams racing under the colours of white, red, blue and green. In the Bardo there is a mosaic showing such a race between four contestants and another shows a charioteer driving a team of horses, who must have been a favourite of the day for his name is given as Eros. It was a sport that had a devoted following and, like politics, it divided the populace into a fervent allegiance to their favourite colours. Not only were they not averse to expressing their rivalry in epithets such as, 'Trip them up, let them not win the race', but they also idolised certain charioteers who became very wealthy, attained a large following and a great deal of notoriety. One of them was Scorpianus who owned a large villa in what was then a very select area and, what is more, he had the foresight to leave his name inscribed on one of his mosaic floors.

Near the Tunis road lie the remains of the amphitheatre which was another popular centre of entertainment for the Carthaginians. This was the scene of many bloody combats between the gladiators, spectacles involving the bestiarii (*Ill. 55*) and the violent deaths of numerous Christian martyrs. St Perptua and her companion St Felicity were condemned by the courts in Carthage for not recognising the cult of the Emperor and making the required oblation. They met their deaths in the arena, savaged by wild animals, and an inscription in Carthage records the event.

Carthage was also renowned for its teachers, one of the most respected being Sulpicius Apollonaris, and for the reputation of its university which compared well with that of Athens and Rome. Many notable Africans began their education here and a number of them went on to those other universities to complete their postgraduate studies. Amongst those who achieved fame and distinction, apart from Apuleius, was the poet Florus, who held public readings of his works in the squares of

53 *The Roman houses between the Antonine Baths and the theatre at Carthage were decorated with fine mosaics and carvings. This column has a vine entwined around it and a man standing on the back of an animal to reach the large bunches of grapes.*

Carthage, and also won the literary prize in Rome. This unfortunately was withheld from him, for the Emperor considered him a provincial upstart and insisted that the reward should go to a candidate from Italy. He did, however, at a later date make a name for himself in Rome in the field of rhetoric. There was also the poet Cornutus and the lawyers Cornelius Fronto and Salvius Julianus and, of course, the renowned Tertullian who also studied law in Rome before becoming one of the most renowned clerics of his time. He was born in Carthage in AD 153 of Punic forebears, and married a Christian girl before he himself became converted. He was very outspoken in his writings and in AD 197 he published his *Apologia* in Carthage. He was not loth to expound his decided views, and, after his conversion, he had a marked influence on the doctrine of the Church. But the one who towered above them all was undoubtedly St Augustine. It is chiefly due to him that the liturgy of the Middle Ages is written in Latin and not Greek, for in the latter tongue he was not at all fluent.

Though Carthage was renowned for its buildings, its elegance and those citizens of note who found fame in the arts and in law, at the other end of the spectrum it was also renowned for its young male prostitutes who, over the years, had managed to gain a reputation throughout the Mediterranean, a reputation that used to be the prerogative of the 'Corinthian Girls' from Acro Corinth. St Augustine in his later years, after being ordained Bishop of Hippo, made frequent visits to Carthage and mentions the young children who were abandoned by their parents, the street cleaners attending to the drains, wives who did not trust their spouses, and the husbands who beat ther wives for looking too avidly at other men. A little to the west of Carthage and not far from the shore are the ruins of the Basilica of St Crispin. Its seven aisles are indicative of its original grandeur and it is a reminder of that period of the Donatist squabbles that beset the Christian Era in North Africa.

Several important roads centred on Carthage, among them the east-west coastal road of Nerva and the great Via Hadriana. This last was a highway, six metres wide, that left Carthage to follow the eastern bank of the Medjerda river before it branched south-east to go through the extensive and fertile wheat growing districts on the way to the important cities of Dougga and Musti, then on to Maktar. The greatest development for the farming community was in the second century. The roads that had originally been built for military purposes were now beginning to influence the agricultural potential and the prosperity of the farmers; they were being linked up and extended by a series of minor roads. Produce from the Berber holdings could now be brought more easily to the markets of the smaller towns that had sprung up and tradesmen came and settled near the veterans' colonies to provide a service and earn a living. The names of some of these early towns are still reflected in the towns that flourish today. Souk-El-Khemisis, or Thursday Market, is one example, situated on the road to Bulla Regia; Souk-El-Arba, or Wednesday Market, is another example. Many of the country towns in Europe also have their individual market days and this is especially

54 *The North African lion was a fierce beast and much in demand in the circus. He was also a favourite motif for furniture, especially the arms and legs of chairs, as well as making a support, as here, for stone bench ends and tables.*

noticeable around Lake Garda in Italy where the towns around the Lake have their own market day so arranged that the traders can take their stalls and wares to each in rotation.

Egypt had supplied Rome with much of her grain requirements since the time of Julius Caesar, but in the first and second centuries AD the Capital depended far more on the shipments from North Africa, which could total as much as half a million tons, enough to supply the requirements of Rome for eight months of the year. The shipments from Carthage made up the annona, or tax, which was calculated and levied by the assessors on the estates and the Berber smallholdings throughout North Africa. Once, during the reign of Nero in AD 68, the Capital experienced great apprehension, panic and near riot, when Clodius Macer, who was then Proconsul in Africa, was in dispute with the Emperor and held back for some months in the port of Carthage the 3000 grain ships which regularly supplied Rome.

Most of the large estates were situated in the fertile grain growing districts, and in many instances were owned by the Imperial Household or by the wealthy absentee landlords. They were worked almost entirely with slave labour supervised by estate managers and there is a reference to this in the *Satyricon* of Petronius, written in the time of Nero. Gaius

55 Detail from a large mosaic which shows bestiarii fighting leopards. Unusually, both animals and attackers are named in the mosaic. Sousse Museum.

Petronius was a close friend of the Emperor and his book (like the *Golden Ass*) gives a unique insight into the ribald life and the excesses in Rome at that time. For a period he was the Proconsul in Bythinia but was later compelled to commit suicide when Nero turned against him, believing in the slanders of a jealous rival. In the book the nouveau riche Emolpus, an old man, is described as having thirty million sesterces invested in farms in North Africa and such an army of slaves on his estates in Numidia that they could have captured Carthage with a minimum of trouble.

In time, however, the employment of slaves on these estates was not looked upon at all favourably by Rome; also, they were beginning to be more difficult to obtain so that the estates had in some cases to be leased to a head lessor. He could then sublet the holdings to peasant farmers on the understanding that they were answerable to the home farm for six days' free labour a year, as well as their share of the annona. Their contribution, as stipulated in the Mancian Law, was 'One third of the wheat from the threshing floor, one third of the barley from the threshing floor, one fourth of the beans, one third of the wine from the vat, one third of the oil from the press, and one sextarius of honey from each hive'.

Though the tenant farmers were required by law to give only six days' free labour to the estate home farms, they were often forced to do more. An inscription near Souk-El Khemis shows how those who worked the small holdings on the Saltus Burunitanus Estate, run by the bailiff Allius Maximus, won the day. They had for some time been forced to work more than the statutory six days and, on refusal to do more, were arrested by the local troops of the legion and severely beaten. It was an estate that had belonged to the Imperial Household, so they sent a petition to Commodus, the ultimate authority, who gave the following ruling: 'In view of the law laid down in the Lex Hadriana, it is my decision that the procurators shall not demand more than thrice two days work lest any unjust exaction be made on you', i.e. by the bailiff.

The procurators were the officials responsible for the administration and the collection of the annona from the estates and farms to send to Rome; in this case they were working hand in glove with the bailiff to step up production. The names of some of the procurators are known. Marcus Vettius Latro from Thuburbo Maius did a stint in the Third Augustan before working in the port of Ostia. He was then procurator of Sicily and Mauretania before he came back to North Africa, and was thus well acquainted with the grain trade. Another, Titus Flavius Macer, once successfully administered the gathering of the extra grain supplies which were demanded from North Africa to make up the deficit in Rome, which was due to the failure of the Egyptian harvest. He was a native of Haidra, owned property there, and was appointed as a procurator to the Imperial Household estates at nearby Tebessa and Hippo. He was also the local administrator of the Musulamii tribe and he could very well have had some previous family connections with them. Most of the land in this region in the past had belonged to the Musulamii tribe and after the defeat of Tacfarinas much of it was confiscated.

Some of the estates in this area are well documented. The Saltus Massipianus was an Imperial estate near Haidra where the tenants had developed their holdings at their own expense, often to the extent of putting up new farm buildings. Two other large estates were in private hands, one belonging to the senator Lucius Africanus and the other to Valeria Aticilla. In relation to these estates held by the wealthy in Rome, there is a documented occasion from the time of Nero, confirmed by Pliny, when six senators who owned vast estates in the area were put to death by the Emperor on the pretext that they were employing unauthorised slave labour; in actuality Nero's object was to confiscate the lot for himself.

Agriculture in Italy had, in part, fallen on hard times and this meant that in order to protect the small farmer in Italy the cultivation of the olive and the vine in North Africa had to be severely restricted. History would seem to have repeated itself with the policies of the present Common Market!

Hadrian reversed this edict, directing that as much land as possible that was not already under cultivation should be opened up. It was one of the decisions he took during his visit to Africa in AD 125. The edict regarding the derelict land enabled prospective farmers, apart from those who already worked their holdings on the estates where they had security of tenure, to take over and develop those areas which were lying waste. They thereby acquired squatter's rights and were considered to be the owners of the land they had reclaimed. Wooded areas were cleared and tracts of hillside terraced to hold rainwater and prevent it flushing into the valleys below. The terraces were planted with olive trees, vines and fruit. To establish these new ventures, and to give these small entrepreneurs a start, they were excused their taxes for some years until their trees and holdings were fully productive. The olive did not need much water for growth, thus it was particularly suitable for the dryer climate of Tripolitania where large groves were planted.

These farmers were not the only peasants to be reckoned with. There were also those large itinerant bands who, having no fixed abode, travelled from estate to estate to help with the harvests for a daily wage. They were the equivalent of the gipsies who, in days gone by, migrated to the hopfields and the fruit farms in England for the season's picking. They lived in the fields during the harvest, very often in huts of straw (*Ill. 56*), and whole families did likewise in Turkey before the relatively recent advent of the John Dere combine harvester. There is an inscription in the Louvre which tells of an itinerant worker from Maktar, who spent twenty years as the leader of such a group that toured the estates of Numidia to help with the harvests, an occupation he followed until he had saved enough to buy his own property, make himself independent and become a respectable citizen. It was a way of life centuries old, that one could see throughout Africa and the Middle East not so many years ago; especially in Palestine in the Plains of Esdraelon, where the primitive plough made in the souks of Nazareth used to be yoked to a camel or a donkey, or to both. The harvests were reaped by

hand with a sickle or scythe, as they are today on the banks of the Nile in Upper Egypt by the fellaheen; a way of life that has now practically disappeared.

Dougga, Musti and Maktar

Dougga, the ancient Thugga (*Ill. 57*), and Musti were two of the largest towns on the Via Hadriana which went through the grain belt east of Carthage. Within a thirty-mile radius of these two towns there are the ruins of ten smaller towns and each, no doubt, had its own market day. Dougga was originally Punic in origin and was included in the territory that Caesar had designated at the end of the Civil War as Africa Nova. At

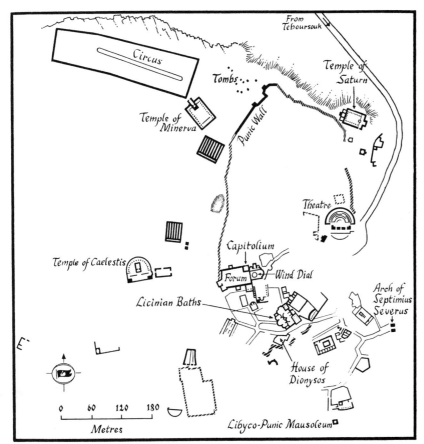

one time it was the home of Masinissa, and had at that time a large Numidian population, but during the first and second centuries AD it developed into a provincial capital with a population of five thousand.

Situated on the top of the hill the Capitol stands well up above the centre of the town which spreads out below it and down along the hillside. If one approaches the town from the direction of Musti its commanding and arresting position can be appreciated; it is very reminiscent of those hill towns in Umbria that are built on the tops of high hills with their churches dominant at the highest point.

The oldest monument in the area dates from the third century BC and is the mausoleum dedicated to the Numidian Prince Ateban, son of Iepmatath, son of Pallu, who was probably a contemporary of Masinissa. It is 20 metres high and stands below the brow of the hill on the edge of the Roman town (*Ill. 62*). Near the top of the monument there are some bas reliefs of four-horse chariots with drivers and an inscription (the original now in the British Museum), in Punic and Berber, names Abarish as the architect. It is one of the most important monuments to be found in Tunisia of that period and, on reflection, one realises that in the second century AD when Dougga was a flourishing Roman city, this monument was to them an antique heritage of the past.

In AD 205 Septimius Severus raised Dougga to the status of a Municipium and granted the inhabitants the right to have their own magistrates' courts, together with the authority to promulgate their own laws. To commemorate this event they raised a Triumphal Arch at the entrance to the town and dedicated it to him. Lists of the magistrates that were appointed show that many of them retained the old family Punic names and there are also many Punic reliefs in the town, especially in the Temple of Saturn.

Since the town was built on a steep hillside, it could not follow the grid system of Hippodamus; as a result there are more winding, and what could have been picturesque streets, used solely by pedestrians such as one can see in many an English country town. The main street has well laid limestone paving, polished and shining, and is bordered with the remains of shop fronts and houses as it winds through the town. This was open to vehicular traffic and one can see the ruts worn by the wheels of the chariots and carts and here, as in Timgad, there are in the street the large square manhole covers, in heavy stone, which give on to the drainage system (*Ill. 58*). The water supplies for the inhabitants and the municipal baths were brought into the town by two aqueducts before being fed into the large cisterns on the outskirts.

58 *A street for pedestrians in Dougga with the paving laid in an unusual herringbone pattern. The square manhole cover in the foreground gave access to the drainage system.*

59 *The temple of Juno Caelestis (the Roman equivalent of the Punic goddess Tanit), was built under Severus Alexander and its elegant columns on their podia were reconstructed by French archaeologists. The temple lies away from the others at Dougga, which cluster around the Capitol.*

Dougga is a city of temples, most of them around the Forum which was rebuilt during the reign of Antoninus Pius and embellished with colonnades of red marble from Smitthus. A second large square, the area Macelli, reached by three steps adjacent to the Capitol, was the 'Place of the Winds', so called because the paved marble court has engraved on it a huge diagram that gives the names and the direction of the four prevailing zephyrs. The finest monument in the city, and possibly in all Tunisia, must be the Capitol itself, with its elegant proportions, built on a slight prominence and reached by a flight of seven steps, its amber stone glowing in the sunlight (Plate 20). Dedicated to Jupiter, Juno and Minerva, it has four fluted columns of the Corinthian order supporting a graceful pediment and, unlike most Capitols which face onto a Forum, this one looks out over the wide ranging views of the town and country – a further example of the flair of the Roman architects when it came to taking full advantage of the site and the environment. Another short flight of steps goes to a smaller colonnaded esplanade and this helps to accentuate the dominance of the Capitol facade.

The other temples, apart from the ruins of the temple of Juno Caelestis (*Ill. 59*), a little way away from the town centre, are clustered around the Capitol, the Forum and the market, which is itself opposite the temple of Mercury, the whole comprising a city centre. They were dedicated to Saturn, Tellus, Fortune, Concordia, Frugifer and Liber Pater, a very motley collection. Adjacent to the last three of these there is a descending staircase giving access to the palaestra and thence to the elegant Licinian Baths.

The theatre was built in AD 168–9 during the reign of Marcus Aurelius (Plate 21). It is a little isolated at the end of a road some distance away from the centre of the town; for the size of the town it was small, having a seating capacity for just on 3500 citizens (*Ill. 60*). Taking into account the multiplicity of temples with their diverse dedications, far more than is found in the average town, and the smallness of the theatre, one wonders if the community tended towards the religious and was not so appreciative of the lighter side of life. If so, this could well be a reflection of a dour Punic ancestry.

The wheat harvests brought a good deal of wealth into the town, a fact reflected in the well-to-do residences, and amongst these large mansions were the House of the Gorgon, and that of the Seasons. It was here that the mosaic of the Four Seasons, now in the Dougga room in the Bardo Museum, was discovered (*Ill. 61*). But most resplendent of all was the House of the Trifolium. It is also the best preserved and was undoubtedly the brothel, judging from the trade mark it once exhibited and which has since been discretely removed. It had a colonnaded court, and leading off this were the entrances to the rooms of the 'ladies' (*Ill. 62*).

Nearby are the Baths of the Cyclops with its palaestra (*Ill. 63*) and the adjacent public latrines in the shape of a horseshoe, with a pedestal hand basin still *in situ* (*Ill. 64*). By comparison with the sumptuous facilities provided in Libya this was a cramped affair with twelve seats, those making use of it having to sit almost knee to knee.

60 *Dougga is built nearly 70 metres above sea level and its theatre is sited so that the auditorium facing the* scaenae frons *looks out over the sharp drop to the valley road below.*

61 *Representations of the Four Seasons, and the farming activities associated with them, were a favourite subject amongst mosaicists in Roman North Africa. This detail of a mosaic from Dougga shows a farm worker gathering the windfalls into a bag at the end of the summer. Bardo Museum, Tunis.*

62 *The House of the Trifolium is one of the finest at Dougga and served as the brothel. The small cubicles for clients opened off the colonnaded court. Beyond, in the distance, can be seen the top of the third-century BC Punic mausoleum of Prince Ateban.*

63 *The palaestra of the Cyclops Baths at Dougga enjoys a magnificent view out over the valley.*

64 *A very convivial atmosphere, strange to modern taste, must have been enjoyed in the horseshoe-shaped multi-seater lavatories in the Cyclops Baths at Dougga. A water channel ran beneath the feet of the occupants and there is a hand basin still on its pedestal in the centre of the wall.*

The Triumphal Arch at the further end of the town (*Ill. 65*) is in a better state of preservation than that of Septimius Severus, and through it went the road to the splendid Temple of Juno Caelestis built in the centre of a large open court (*Ill. 59*). Both the temple and the arch were erected between AD 222–35 during the reign of Severus Alexander, and the arch has his dedication inscribed on one of the pillars.

Another interesting inscription from the town is dedicated to the Emperor Augustus and relates to some improvements carried out by one of the rich citizens. It goes, 'To Imperator Caesar Augustus, son of divine Augustus Pontifex Maximus, in his 38th year of tribunician power, consul five times: Lucius Bucco, son of Lucius, of the tribe Arnensis, Duumvir; made this dedication, Lucius Postumius Chius, son of Gaius of the tribe Arnensis, Patron of the community in the name of himself and his sons, Firmus and Rufus, paved the forum and the area in front of the Temple of Caesar and had the altar of Augustus, the Temple of Saturn and the arch built at his own expense'.

65 *The Arch of Severus Alexander at Dougga built between AD 222–235 is well preserved and quite simple in its lines compared to some of the earlier, more grandiose, examples of Trajan and Septimius Severus.*

Musti

Musti lies eight miles east of Dougga in the centre of the grain belt but it is not on such a spectacular site, though it does have extensive views over the wheat plains. It was built on a slight rise at the foot of the hills and once covered an area of fourteen hectares, but little is left of the city today. The small triumphal arch, in those days the Carthage gate, was the original entrance to the town; now it stands alone and forlorn, separated from the ruins of the old town by the modern highway. What is left is centred around the façades of the temples of Ceres, Pluto and Apollo, but the most striking feature is the street next to the temples that went up through the town to a Forum. On either side of the entrance to the street are fine arches in a yellow sandstone which led into a colonnade of shops, so intact are they that one feels that they could, with little restoration, be taken on to the books of an estate agent (*Ill. 66*). They evoke the Georgian period and are very reminiscent of some of the smaller streets in Bath. The street itself is well paved and scoured to help pedestrians walk on the well polished surface; here too one finds those ruts in the stone that, over the years, were worn by the wheels of the carts.

In the square beyond the street are the remains of an oil press, and in

66 *The paved street with its adjacent arcade of shops is remarkably well preserved at Musti, giving the impression that they have only just been vacated.*

another part of the town can be seen what was once a small factory for the production of oil in quantity, with a press in its original place. Not far from the temples is the large colonnaded court of another delightful villa, not unlike the House of the Trifolium in Dougga – and it served the same purpose – for in this case the virile sign of the establishment is set up for all to see. The Christian Basilica near the square has sunk into the floor of the small baptistry an unusual round font, not the usual cruciform shape, which was filled from a large tall water tank built into the corner of the wall and, amazingly, this too is completely intact.

Maktar

Forty miles south from Musti lies Maktar, another provincial capital situated at a thousand metres on the dome of a hill only a little distance from the ancient and picturesque Berber village of La Kesra, also up in the hills. This city was also of Punic origin and for a long time was another bastion of the Numidian kings; in 146 BC it became a haven for those refugees who fled from the Carthaginian Wars. It was also the headquarters of the younger Scipio before the Battle of Zama which ended with the defeat of Hannibal. The site of the conflict was in the open country a little off the road from Maktar to Siliana.

One can see that Punic culture became well established in Maktar after the influx of the refugees, for they built a tophet sanctuary and a temple in the town, and then followed their Punic way of life well on into the Roman period. The numerous Punic stelae with their foreboding figures in bas relief testify to Plutarch's assessment of them when he called them 'a dour and gloomy race'. There are a few stelae from the Christian period and one portrays a rather hefty angel, obviously male for he is unclothed and looks as if he could not take off from the ground, let alone sit on a cloud (*Ill. 67*). An obituary preserved in the museum engraved on a small headstone is well worth mentioning. It records that Laurentius passed on after 'living 31 years, 8 months, and three hours' – someone in his family was keeping a close count. The Vandals too, as far as they were concerned, had a rewarding time here knocking the noses off the Roman statues. The Triumphal Arch of the city is now at the crossroads leading to the present town, a pleasant place built on the opposite hill; and not far from the arch are the remains of the tophet sanctuary built by the refugees.

One has to climb the hill past the small amphitheatre to reach the Forum which was laid out on its highest aspect (Plate 22); this was the centre of the town with extensive views over the other hill. The broad and open expanse of the Forum and the brilliant white glare of the paving is almost startling in its impact when one first sets foot on it. The bases of the columns that once supported the colonnade are here, as is the fine Arch of Trajan standing alone and dominating the scene. The surrounding walls and shops have gone, for it used to be the entrance and exit to the precinct.

Beyond the arch the road went through the town past the Basilica of

67 *An angel on a Christian tombstone from Maktar still has a very pagan appearance, especially in the downturned torch he holds that is an attribute of Mithras' companion Cautopates.*

Hildeguns and on down the hill to the large baths. These were built in the late second century AD and must have been widely renowned, judging from the restored entrance hall with its rows of fine arches and the many beautiful mosaic floors. There is an old Numidian Forum without colonnades, for these were a feature peculiar to the Roman Forum, and a Punic temple that was put up in earlier years by the Carthaginian refugees and later on converted by the Christians into a church. A ruined temple of Bacchus is not far off, two distinctly opposing cults almost on each other's doorstep. Beyond was the Capitol and a second baths, all now just a heap of rubble.

Quite the most interesting and unique part of the town however is the Schola of the Juvenes which was founded in the first century AD, its activities being recorded in a later inscription to the Emperor Domitian. It was a youth organisation which undertook various duties such as policing the town almost like vigilantes. They also had periods of military training to fit them for service as auxilary troops, not unlike the old Officers' Training Corps which used to be a part of life in some of the public schools. Their main duty, however, was to supervise the collection of the Annona which the procurators had levied on the surrounding farms. It was stored in a series of stone bins – they are still intact (*Ill. 68*) – and the grain measures were let into the sills of the

68 *Grain bins in the Schola of the Juvenes at Maktar where the grain, the Anonna levied by the procurators and collected from the local farmers, was stored.*

windows of a building with a clover leaf apse (*Ill. 69*). Here the grain was poured to the requisite level before being transferred to the bins to remain in bond and await transport to Carthage and shipment to Rome. It was the farmer from Maktar who spent twenty years of his life with his band of labourers, going from farm to farm to help with the harvests till he had saved enough to buy his own property. It is a pity that the inscription in the Louvre does not record his name.

The palaestra (Plate 23) which was a part of the complex of the Schola of the Juvenes has around it some well balanced and proportioned columns with a pleasing vista and, though at a later date a small basilica was built in a part of the structure, it does not appear to have taken anything away from the overall design.

69 *The apsidal-ended Schola of the Juvenes at Maktar with grain bins for the Annona let into the sills beneath the arches (see also Plate 23).*

El Djem

El Djem, the ancient Thysdrus, is the last of the agricultural towns of note and is situated south of Sousse on a fertile plateau. Though the sites of many of the old Roman cities are impressive, this one is spectacular. As one approaches the present town the massive amphitheatre, the sixth largest of the Roman world, rises above the plateau, magnificent in its isolation for the surrounding Roman town has virtually gone. By the third century AD it had a population of ten thousand and was probably the richest city in North Africa, a fact born out by the many beautiful mosaics that have been recovered from the houses and villas, many of them having courtyards, colonnades and well kept gardens watered from large cisterns. The themes of the mosaics (*Ills. 70, 71*) embrace all the aspects of their life from religion to their love of food, not to mention their various amorous peccadilloes that were recorded for all to see.

The main prosperity of the town came from the 37,000 acres of olive groves that Hadrian ordered planted, and today the groves stretch to the horizon. In the third century the owners of these large estates had imposed on them an extortionate land tax and they had, in consequence, revolted. It was this revolt in AD 238 that brought about the election of Gordian as Emperor at the age of eighty-eight, for he was at that time the proconsul and living in the district.

The amphitheatre here is the only one left standing in North Africa, and it would have been in an even better state of preservation had the stone not been pillaged to build the local town (Plate 24). It is oval in shape, 175 × 135 metres, and had three tiers of seats with arcades. These could seat the 30,000 spectators who entered the vaulted galleries from

70 *A graphic study of life in the wild is seen on this mosaic from El Djem, where a tiger leaps onto the haunches of a wild ass whilst its companion makes good its escape. El Djem Museum.*

the stairways. The Emperor, or his substitute, sat in the shade, and it was not unlike the Spanish bull ring in layout. Below the arena one finds the usual passages and rooms where the gladiators and the beasts, the criminals and the Christian martyrs, used to await their turn to figure in the spectacles (Plate 25). A statue of Marcus Aurelius once stood in the middle of one of the underground passages and the gladiators were obliged to file around it on their way to the arena. Some of them survived so many bouts and had such charisma that they too became very popular and, like the successful charioteers, enjoyed a notoriety that is given to many football players and transient pop stars of today. Numerous graffiti detailing their exploits can be read on the walls of Pompeii, though none seem to have survived in El Djem.

The gladiatorial shows were immensely popular throughout the Roman world; the spectacles of mutilation in the arena and the fate of the Christians were much in demand by the populace who had a contempt for death. A floor in one of the villas in what was once a residential district shows Christians being forced, almost naked, into the arena by gladiators, and kept there whilst being attacked by leopards. Another mosaic from Zliten in Libya, which is in the Tripoli Museum, also shows Christian martyrs being pushed into the arena to face the beasts; they are bound to upright stakes which were mounted on small two wheeled carts.

Gladiators were often recruited from the ranks of condemned criminals or slaves, and riotous feasts were held by them in the evening

71 One of the most famous mosaics from El Djem, possibly from the whole of Roman North Africa, shows Ulysses, tightly bound to the mast of his ship, resisting the Sirens' song whilst his sailors row resolutely onward, saved by the wax blocking their ears. Bardo Museum, Tunis.

before the shows. One of these occasions is illustrated in a mosaic from El Djem, now in the Bardo Museum. It shows those who are due to take part in the coming spectacles the next day having a noisy meal, the humorous inscription below saying, 'Silentium dormiant Tauri' – 'Silence, let the bulls sleep'. The Emperor Commodus fancied himself as a gladiator and took part in many of the games, but it is very evident that he was never so unfortunate as to lose an encounter, though he did also pit himself against the wild beasts in the arena, apparently quite successfully. He was never more happy than when in the company of gladiators and, as has been said, would attend formal meetings of the Senate dressed as one, much to the Senators' disgust.

Bulls and bears were the least exotic of the animals used in the amphitheatre. Giraffes, rhinoceroses, hippopotami, leopards, lions and tigers all took part and the great majority of them were shipped from Africa to the theatres of the Empire. Lions and tigers were commonplace in North Africa and Pliny has confirmed that six hundred were used in one spectacle in the first century BC, which could refer to Caesar's Triumph. Capturing the animals and transporting them to the arenas was big business. The method of netting them can be seen in the mosaics at Piazza Armerina in Sicily and, as a result of this wholesale slaughter, many species became extinct in Africa. These animals are constantly represented in the mosaics, but rarely is the camel pictured. The desert tribes in Libya used them at an early date, but they did not become commonplace in the Maghreb till the late Roman period.

Another of the important roads built by Trajan went west from Carthage to follow the Medjerda river. To cross the smaller Beja river he built a three-arched bridge of such a solid construction that, like that of Severus in Commagene, it is still in use today. The road is picturesque with lovely views; in those days it passed through five towns, including Souk El Khemis, before it reached more vast wheat plains and the town of Bulla Regia. The plains are so flat one feels that the bubble in a spirit level would not lose its tranquility wherever it was placed. In Roman times the land was devoted to cereal crops, but in the summer, for there was little shade, the climate was so hot it was like a frying pan.

Bulla Regia was another royal city of the Numidian kings; it was a favourite place of residence and particularly liked by Hierbas who spent whatever time he could there. In order to compete with the fierce summer climate many of the residences of the wealthy land owners were built on two levels, the one below ground being used during the hot season (Plate 12). A villa in the Via dell'Abbondanza in Pompeii was built in this fashion, but there it is the exception.

Many of the mosaic floors in the villas here are also well preserved, the finest being in the Villa des Mosaics, but those that were in the Palais de Chasse are now in the Bardo. In this villa the smoke marks are evident on the kitchen walls and the lower rooms are cool in the hottest weather and well lit from the shafts that go up to the street level. In one of the villas on the ground level is a small closet complete with a two-seated latrine and a mosaic floor which demonstrates that the domestic facilities here were in

72 *Even in private houses some lavatories were multi-seated, admittedly only a two-seater here in a villa at Bulla Regia.*

no way primitive (*Ill. 72*). There is in fact evidence that during the winter, which could be cold, some of the underground rooms could be warmed with hot air circulated through ducts which one can see in the angle of the walls.

The streets are well preserved and retain their paving, thus giving an overall impression of how the town looked when inhabited, but the Capitol and the Forum are featureless though the baths retain some of their original rooms and mosaic floors. The theatre is small but well proportioned and still has its tiers of seats and the stage, but unfortunately this can often be covered with a layer of mud some inches thick after the autumn rains. Not far from the theatre is a bath in the shape of a clover leaf covered in mosaic which seems to have been reserved solely for the use of the players. The water that was needed to supply these amenities was derived from a catchment area and stored in numerous cisterns around the outskirts.

From Bulla Regia the road goes on for a further fifteen miles to the Imperial quarries at Simitthus, now known as Chemtou. These were worked to produce the prized red Numidian marble that was so greatly admired and valued by the Emperors. It was Hadrian who particularly liked the colour of the stone and he built the 'transport highway' from the quarries to the port of Thabraca, some forty miles away, solely to ship the great quantities he required for decorating the villa he had under construction at Tivoli in the Alban Hills outside Rome.

An interesting inscription comes from Simitthus and relates to a legionary of the Third Augustan Legion, whose unit had been stationed in the Bulla Regia district. It states: 'Lucius Flaminius, son of Decimus, of the Tribe Arnensis, soldier of the Legion III Augusta, of the century of Julius Longus, chosen in a levy by Marcus Silanus, served 29 years on garrison duty when he was killed in the Philomusian range by the enemy in battle, lived dutifully 40 years, lies here'. If Lucius at the age of forty had served twenty-nine years, he must have joined the Legion when he was eleven years of age! Here again the tribe of Arnensis is mentioned though Lucius was obviously not wealthy, nor could he have been in the same social class as he who paved the Forum at Dougga. He was, however, just as proud of his achievements.

From Thabraca the main coastal road of Nerva goes east to Libya and west to Algeria to the ancient cities of Iol Caesarea, Juba's old capital and today's Cherchel, thence on to Tipasa. In Cherchel there are only the scanty remains of this once splendid capital, which it must have been judging from the length of Juba's reign, his intellectual capacity and the art treasures he amassed.

There is a great deal more at Tipasa, once a Roman port that had a considerable trade which Juba must have encouraged. The Decumanus Maximus, some 350 feet long, is still apparent and went through the town from the elliptical amphitheatre to the Iol Caesarea Gate. On the way it passed two temples, one on either side of the road, then the Nymphaeum, and thence to the theatre. One of the temples had a paved court, a monumental staircase, a portico and then another flight of steps. It was an important structure that was later turned into a church, like many others in North Africa in the Christian Era. The Forum, the Capitol and the Law Courts are all ruined. The theatre, however, was built on an artificially raised mound, one of the rare instances where this method was employed to obtain height, and it could seat up to a thousand at a time in the auditorium. Part of the economy depended on a factory that had been built near the shore to produce the garum sauce manufactured from the salted entrails of fish. Apart from local consumption this was exported in great quantities, for the Romans considered it to be a great delicacy.

An influence which went back to the town's Punic origins lingered on and remained a cult that was followed by a section of the populace even during the first century AD, for numerous stelae have been found pointing to the fact that considerable sections of the populace still continued to worship the goddess Tanit. In the later centuries the Christians built two great churches, the largest on the highest point of the western cliff overlooking some private baths and the sea. It was a massive edifice measuring 52 by 42 metres, and had nine naves.

Another basilica, which contained the tomb of St Salsa and was dedicated to her, was put up on the peak of the promontory named after her, and this became a place of pilgrimage. She was a Christian girl who, it was said, objected to the pagan faiths that were tolerated in the city and felt so strongly about their presence that she took it upon herself to break their idols. This was obviously not a popular course of action, however strongly she might have felt about the issue, and she was stoned to death for her intolerance. Her body was thrown into the sea but the sea refused to accept it and, in order to give it rest, it had to be recovered and interred with the proper rites. Apparently when the tomb was opened many decades later it contained, not the bones of a young girl, but those of an old woman. A case of the germ of truth in a legend not strictly bearing out the facts.

9

The Rise of Christianity in North Africa

The Romans were, on the whole, very broadminded regarding the different cults and religions practised in the colonies and those parts of the Empire which they had taken over and conquered. In the process of Romanisation, many gods were absorbed into the pantheon of the Roman deities and had temples built to them in Rome. The Egyptian cults of Isis and Serapis and the Persian cult of Mithras, a deity very popular with the legions, were probably those that had most impact. There are temples dedicated to Isis and Serapis in Pompeii and Ephesus, as well as one dedicated to Mithras in London. In Ephesus the indigenous cult of the mother goddess Cybele was, over the years, combined with that of Diana of the Ephesians.

The Syrian cult of Baal, which centred on Carthage, still persisted in a muted form, though child sacrifice could still take place quietly in some remote country districts. It had been actively suppressed by the Romans and still was proscribed when brought to light. The state cult of the Emperor, however, was the most important. It kept the peoples of the Empire together and sacrifices and libations had to be observed as homage before official functions and other important occasions.

The Jews had come to North Africa early on and had their ghettos in most of the big cities, especially Alexandria and Cyrene; and it is more than likely that Christianity was brought with the travellers from Rome and the east who had embraced the faith. Christianity spread throughout North Africa far quicker than it did in other parts of the Empire, and it was the scene of many martyrdoms suffered under the persecutions. The main bone of contention was the fact that the Christians would not recognise the cult of the Emperor. Not recognising the other religions practised throughout the Empire did not matter, but that of the Emperor was the most important. Nevertheless, the persecutions were not systematic, but arose at the whim of the emperor concerned, or they were often dependent on the attitude adopted by the provincial governors.

Pliny, when Governor of Bithynia in Asia Minor under Trajan, wrote to him asking for directives as to what line to adopt with the Christians.

He was told that he was not to actively entrap or seek them out, nor to listen to malicious denunciations, but when properly accused they were to be dealt with through the courts, and this only if they refused to recant or to make the required sacrifice to the Emperor's cult. It was this sacrifice that was the stumbling block. It was a pagan way of recognising the Emperor to be the all-powerful Head of State and a ritual somewhat akin to the singing of a national anthem. The mad Caligula really considered himself to be a god on earth, which the Roman populace derided, but not openly. It was Nero who, wishing to lay the blame for the fire of Rome on the shoulders of the Christians, brought about the first major persecutions resulting in the loss of many lives and the martyrdoms of St Peter and St Paul.

The first Christian martyrs in North Africa were seven men and five women, inhabitants of Scilli, who, having refused to sacrifice to the Emperor, were arraigned before the Proconsul Saturnius in Carthage. He gave them every opportunity to mitigate their predicament, but they remained uncompromising and adamant, so they went to their deaths in spite of the fact that in every other respect they were good citizens and well-thought-of members of the community. The trials of those accused were recorded by the court secretaries known as the *acta* and by the contemporary accounts of those other Christians who witnessed the events; they are also substantiated in the accounts of the martyrs themselves that were written before they went to their deaths in the arena.

There is an inscription on a tomb in Carthage dedicated to the martyrs Saturus, Saturninus (a name as common as Smith in North Africa), Secundus, the two slaves Revocatus and Felicity, and the most distinguished of them all, St Perpetua. They were all brought before the court at Carthage in AD 203. St Perpetua came from a wealthy pagan family, was twenty-two years old and married with a young son. At her trial she and the others refused to be shaken, but her father who attended the hearing exhorted her repeatedly to sacrifice for the prosperity of the Emperor, to respect his grey hairs and to think of her son. Apparently he made so much noise he had to be removed and he was flogged outside for contempt of court. St Perpetua has herself left a record of the proceedings, *The Passione*, and this describes how the Procurator Hilarion pleaded with her and the others to offer just one sacrifice to the Emperor to spare herself and the family, but they all refused. They were condemned to be thrown into the arena on the day of the public games on 7 March AD 203. The evening before they all cheerfully attended a public banquet which was the preliminary to the forthcoming festivities, eagerly watched by the Carthaginian populace. The manner of their deaths from a leopard, bear and other beasts has been described by an eye witness. It is difficult to fathom the mentality of a public who could demand such a spectacle, though no doubt we have just a glimpse of it in the Spanish bullfight; in the latter case of course, the one without the fighting chance being the bull.

Their trial was held during the visit of Septimius Severus and Julia

Domna to Leptis. Severus is credited with having issued a decree instigating a period of Christian persecution, whereby believers were actively sought out and brought before the courts whenever possible. Yet Tertullian, who was the most strident, vehement and outspoken of them all, and who published his *Apologia* in Carthage in AD 197, was not brought to book. Neither were any of those employed openly in the household of Julia, nor was the Christian brother of St Perpetua.

It was during the reign of Septimius Severus in AD 189 that Victor I was elected Pope in Rome, the first African to take office which he held until his death in AD 199. After the death of Severus and up to the year AD 248, Christianity spread rapidly throughout North Africa, even reaching into the oases. In that year St Cyprian became the first and most notable Bishop of Carthage. He also was from a pagan background and was converted in his forties. Indeed he proved to be so able that within two to three years of his conversion, he was elected a Bishop and he immediately began to establish the Church on a firm basis. St Cyprian had not long been in office, however, when the Decian persecutions began and it was the same old story. Decius, when he came to power, declared that the Christians must make the required oblation to the state cult of the Emperor, a ritual that had been glossed over in the past years. Only one act of sacrifice was needed to absolve them from further ritual and those who panicked and conformed were granted a certificate to that effect by the courts. Those who refused went to prison and had their property and goods confiscated, these backsliders being known as the *lapsi*.

Happily for the Christians, Decius did not survive for long and on his death St Cyprian, who had removed himself to a remote part of the country when the trouble broke out, returned to Carthage. He then found that internecine quarrels had produced a schism within the Church regarding the *lapsi*, who had not been forgiven by those who had stuck it out and gone to prison for their faith. The *lapsi* had been readmitted to the Church and had often been baptised by those priests who supported the 'Schism'. It was St Cyprian's view that these baptisms were illegal, unfortunately a view that was not upheld by the Bishops of Rome. It all boiled down at the time to Church discipline and, to settle the question, St Cyprian convened a conference in AD 256 that was to be held in Carthage. The Emperor Valerian began his persecutions not long after the conference had ended, and they proved to be even more severe than those of Decius. All the hierachy of the Church, the bishops, the clergy and those who refused to sacrifice, were either executed or exiled to the mines. St Cyprian too was beheaded in the countryside outside Carthage on 14 September AD 258. His death was followed some months later by the execution of two of the Numidian bishops, and then by two other members of the Church, St James and St Marian. This last act soon led to a holocaust of the Christians who were rounded up in great numbers and slaughtered wholesale.

The famous Third Augustan Legion had been disbanded by Gordian III in AD 238, but in view of the uprisings that had subsequently occurred on the frontiers, it had to be reformed in AD 253. Intermittent uprisings still broke out until the reigns of Diocletian and Maximian in AD 248, by which time Volubilis in Mauretania had been abandoned. It was about this time that the stability of the economy began to suffer and rampant inflation resulted, which Diocletian endeavoured to solve by debasing the currency. This had its effects on Africa. Diocletian had recently moved his capital to Nicomedia in Bithynia and to find the large sums of money he required, taxes had to be raised and these had a knock-on effect throughout the colonies. In Africa, those in the towns who could not pay their way fled to the country. Those small farmers in the country who failed through bad harvests and escalating bills went bankrupt and had their holdings taken over by the larger estates.

To try and control the situation, Diocletian imposed a prices and incomes policy which was displayed in the markets throughout the Empire and the penalties for its non-observance were severe. One can still see a full copy of the decree incised on the walls of the marcellum, or meat market in Cavdarhisar, a town in Turkey not far from Nicomedia. It lays down the wages for all classes of occupation, such as librarian, assistant librarian, carpenter and so on. It also indicates the prices to be paid for all commodities, even to the cost of a length of black cloth manufactured from the wool of the famous black sheep of Laodicea. No one was allowed to change their occupation or trade, which had to be followed by subsequent members of the family. In Africa, it turned the citizens into two classes, the very rich and the poor, and it is from this period in the early fourth century that many of the great villas, estates and the later fine mosaics date. The villas were extensive, often with their own private baths, and were run by the lord of the manor, who employed all those necessary to maintain the domain, such as farmers and artisans. The great estates in England of the seventeenth and eighteenth centuries worked on the same principle, whereby those in the villages depended largely for their living on the work and the bounty provided by their lord of the manor.

By this time Christianity had practically taken over North Africa, having been embraced by all and sundry, including many peasants in the remoter parts of Numidia. The bishops by now were far more numerous and had their own well organised parishes, and it was into this state of affairs that Diocletian unleashed his persecutions in AD 303. It was not only the clergy who suffered this time, but also the lowly. The churches were closed and the priests required to hand over all their liturgical books to be burnt. If they did not comply they were harshly dealt with and the edict led to more martyrdoms. Many bishops however, including Paulus of Constantine, handed their scriptures over to the courts and thus they became known as the *traditores*, the equivalent of the earlier *lapsi*. But many remained steadfast and this is illustrated by the account of Saturninus, the priest of Arbitina. He, together with his entire congregation of fifty souls, maintained their stance in the courts of Carthage and were all convicted. Their presiding bishop, meanwhile, had handed in his books and remained inviolate.

It was the beginning of the split of the Church into two factions, the Catholics and the Donatists, or broadly speaking, those who had handed over their religious documents, the Catholic-*traditores*, and those who had stuck to their guns and refused to compromise. Over the years, the schism occasioned a great deal of mud-slinging and jockeying for position between the two factions. This even extended to murder on the part of Bishop Purpurus, who quite openly admitted his guilt and defiantly said that he was prepared to do the same again. In AD 312, Caecilian was consecrated Bishop of Carthage on the death of Mensurius, who was one of the *traditores*. He had been the deacon of Mensurius and was heartily disliked for his attitude towards those martyrs who had not compromised, regarding their action as quite idiotic in view of the troubles they had incurred through their stubborness. His appointment was bitterly opposed by the bishops of Numidia. All seventy of them descended on Carthage to protest against it and dethrone him, an action which resulted in one of their party being murdered in the Church. Although they failed to oust Caecilian, they retaliated by electing Majorinus their own Donatist candidate. It came about in a peculiar way. Caecilian had once been exceptionally rude to a wealthy and influential woman called Lucilla, and when the squabble arose she bribed the Donatist faction to elect Majorinus. He had, in fact, very little qualification for the post for up to the time of his consecration he had simply been a member of her household. Carthage now had two bishops, one for each faction, and the seventy (less one) recalcitrant bishops returned to Numidia well satisfied. Majorinus died shortly after being consecrated and Donatus was elected Bishop in his place.

Donatus came from an arid part of the country south of Tebessa almost on the borders of the Sahara and he had fully supported the Numidian bishops against Caecilian. He came to be regarded as the leader of the schism which was named after him, and held office for well on forty years. The violent quarrels over Church discipline continued well into the reign of Constantine the Great, who, much to the chagrin of the Donatists, backed Bishop Caecilian and the Catholics and, to make matters worse, he declared that the Catholics should have what was left of their previously confiscated property returned. The Donatists again protested and both Caecilian and Donatus were invited to Rome to put their case to Pope Militades and a Council of Bishops, all of them supporting Caecilian after much deliberation. By now the Edict of Milan of AD 313 had made Christianity the official religion of the Empire. In AD 314 at the Council of Arles, the Donatists again lost the day and were ordered to hand over their property to the Catholics and to cease functioning as an independent Church. This they refused to do and the Catholics, short of using armed force, could do nothing. The Donatists went from strength to strength building more and more churches; amongst many others they built seventeen in Timgad and one in Tebessa. The Christians came over to them to such an extent that at one time there were 250 Donatist bishops throughout Africa. In AD 330 they had the audacity to forcefully confiscate the Catholic basilica in Carthage for their own use, the Catholics then having to build another for themselves.

Trouble again arose between the two factions in AD 337. The schism attracted more dissension and militancy in an endeavour to persuade the Donatists back into the Catholic tradition. The worst event, however, took place in AD 347 when Macarius was sent from Rome to enforce unity between them. He marched into Numidia to the town of Bagai in the Aures mountains, but before he arrived the Donatists barricaded themselves into the church before sending a party of ten bishops to negotiate with him. They were all tied to posts and flogged and those in the church were massacred. The situation ended with the banishment of Donatus himself, and he remained in exile until he died in AD 355. The Church, however, prospered to the extent that it managed to regain what was left of its property, largely due to the sympathy shown by the administration of Julian the Apostate. It was not the end of the story: the Donatists again turned on the Catholics and more bitter fighting broke out, which continued periodically until the end of the century.

The splendour of Rome in North Africa was breaking up and rapidly becoming a phenomenon of the past. Leptis was devastated by the tribes of the Austurani and the inhabitants turned to Rome for help. This was sent to them with Count Romanus, but he did little and left them to their fate. The olive groves were destroyed and Leptis, Sabratha and Oea gradually succumbed to the sands of the desert, after a very brief respite under the Byzantines.

A revolt broke out in the Kybele mountains in AD 372, led by the prosperous Jubaleni tribe who had the support of the Donatists. It was put down by Theodosius at the gates of Tipasa, but twenty years later it broke out again under Gildo, who was then the leader of the tribe, and he held up the corn supplies to Rome. Once more the Donatists were involved, led by Bishop Optatus of Timgad, and again they were defeated with help from Rome. Optatus paid the extreme penalty and the vast estates of the Jubaleni were confiscated. The revolt arose in the year that St Augustine was consecrated Bishop of Hippo. He was one of the most revered clerics in the history of the Christian church, and one whose influence and teaching did much to shape its future development. He was born in AD 354 into a middle-class family at Thagaste, the son of a pagan father and a Christian mother. He went to school in Madauros (where Apuleius of *The Golden Ass* was born), later going to the University of Carthage where he not only excelled in his studies, but was very promiscuous and enjoyed to the full the good things of life, not unlike many of today's undergraduates. When he was twenty-nine, he went to Rome with his son Adeodatus and his mistress, and there he endeavoured to make a living by teaching. However he found it difficult to make both ends meet, for his pupils were very tardy in settling their fees, if they ever did. Not long after his arrival in Rome he was appointed to a post in Milan. Once he had established himself there he was joined by Monica, his mother. Here he spent some years teaching and became involved with St Ambrose, the Bishop of Milan, who took him under his wing and became the moving spirit in his subsequent career.

After some years Augustine suddenly decided to return to North Africa, a decision his mother welcomed. Unfortunately she died after a short illness in Ostia before they could embark. He returned to Africa in AD 388, and was consecrated Bishop of Hippo in AD 395. The Donatists at the time were very powerful and had just appointed Bishop Petilian in Constantine to oppose the Catholics. Bishop Aurelian of Carthage was the senior cleric to Augustine and the two of them endeavoured over the years to bring the Donatists back to the Catholic tradition. It was a problem that was to remain with Augustine for the rest of his life. His ministry was not confined to the spiritual for he also had a great secular interest in the lives of his parishoners. He acted as an arbitrator in disputes and his writings contain many anecdotes and illustrations of everyday life around him. He mentions the tight-rope walkers, who must have been very popular for Apuleius also refers to them. He talks of those who feared the surgeon's knife, and the man who was cold at night because his mistress would not let him wear clothes. He mentions bird watchers, highway men, the landowners who employed night watchmen to watch their crops, and those who stored their grain in damp bins. He also mentions the barbers, the jealous husbands who beat their wives, and those who taught their pet parrots questionable phrases. It all seems only too familiar, even down to the parrots.

Apart from all this, however, Augustine founded monasteries and supported other such ecclesiastical institutions. The monks came from all walks of life and had to support themselves by work and not on gifts or charity, for he was against those he described as hypocrites who were of no fixed address, had long hair, and wandered the countryside in a monk's habit selling worthless relics. Relics of St Stephen had come to Hippo from Jerusalem and were accredited with healing powers, though St Augustine was not entirely convinced. There was, however, the case of the temblers from Cappadocia who had been cursed by their widowed mother, so that all of them were afflicted with an incessant shaking of the limbs that they could not control. They were so unique they managed to earn a living exhibiting their disability. Paulus and his sister Pallida, two of the family, came to Hippo and began to attend the Church of Saint Augustine. During one of the services Paulus touched the shrine of St Stephen, fell flat on his face in a trance and then got up cured. The congregation were delighted and during the next service whilst listening to a eulogy by St Augustine on the event, Pallida also touched the shrine and she too fell flat on her face and then got up cured. St Augustine is said to have remarked that 'Christian miracles are the work of God helped on by the martyrs'. The many books that he has left to posterity include his two greatest works, *The City of God* and his *Confessions*.

Missionaries left the monastries in an endeavour to convert those in the Donatist strongholds but their verbal propaganda had little effect and the controversy raged throughout the time of Theodosius to continue into the administration of his young sons, the emperors Arcadius and Honorius. The Catholics endeavoured to arraign the Donatists as heretics so that they should come within the law, but the

Donatists retaliated with acts of force perpetrated by the *circumcelliones*, bands of religious fanatics from the peasantry who attacked the Catholic homesteads, setting them on fire and beating up their bishops and clergy whenever they could be ambushed. However, Honorius, in his Edict of Unity in AD 405, outlawed the schism as a heresy and declared that all the Donatist property should be handed over to the Catholics. In spite of the Edict and the fact that they were now open to persecution and imprisonment, the Donatists still persisted to the point that Augustine had to suffer the humiliation of the *circumcelliones* electing their own Bishop right under his nose in Hippo.

In AD 410, he was obliged to seek out the help of Honorius in Ravenna and here he was successful. A Council was convened on 8 June AD 411, and this was attended by St Augustine and his adversary, the Bishop Petilian. The Donatists as usual were recalcitrant, complained that they were the persecuted ones and remained standing throughout the proceedings, in an effort to entirely disassociate themselves from the Council. They lost their case and it was decreed that henceforth Donatism would be a criminal offence. The bishops Macrobius and Petilian left Hippo and Constantine respectively, but they still remained active in the remoter regions of Numidia, where many were brought to trial. In spite of all this, the heresy still flourished in many cities and especially in Timgad.

North Africa was now facing another upheaval, not due this time to the internal religious dissensions, but from the invading Vandals under King Gaiseric. They were the Arian Christian heretics who had crossed over from Gibraltar in August AD 429. Men, women and children, over 100,000 of them, came to confront Count Boniface, whom Procopius considered to be one of the last great Roman soldiers. In spite of help sent by the Empress Galla Placidia from Ravenna (her tomb with its magnificent mosaics is still there), Boniface had to retreat to Hippo, where Augustine died during the siege in AD 430 with the Vandals knocking at the door. Hippo was taken, Count Boniface returned to Italy and, after they had captured Carthage, the Vandals settled themselves in Numidia. Roman influence in North Africa was now at an end. The Vandals dug themselves in to enjoy the way of life created by the Romans – they at once looted the churches of their treasures before they installed their own priests. The life of the indigenous population went on, although many of the Roman landlords were dispossessed in favour of the invaders. The Vandals soon fell into the role of the wealthy patron and to Rome the greatest loss was the supply of corn.

Once established and with the Carthaginian fleet at his disposal – oil was still exported in great quantities – Gaiseric began a series of raids throughout the Mediterranean attacking and looting cities, and burning towns and villages in Sicily and Sardinia. In AD 455 his audacity extended to the looting of Rome but its complete devastation was averted by the forceful personality of Pope Leo. However, all the treasures were taken and amongst them the Menorah, the sacred five-branched candlestick which Titus had taken from the Temple after the Fall of Jerusalem. It can be seen represented amongst the spoils that are shown in the relief on his Triumphal Arch in the Forum in Rome. Towards the end of Gaiseric's career, the local hill tribes and those of the desert gradually overran the old cities, such as Lambaesis and Dougga. Their citizens eventually deserted them and the Catholics were persecuted so viciously that many of them crossed into Spain, whilst in Africa one Vandal king followed another in a confused political climate.

It was Justinian in Constantinople who decided that North Africa should return to the Empire. To this end he sent his most able general, Count Belisarius who, with a considerable force transported in 500 ships, landed in AD 153 in the Gulf of Sirte. The historian Procopius was with him on the expedition acting as his private secretary, and he has left accounts of the invasion. He describes the army, after its landing and advance, camping in the park and the fruit orchards of the palace of Gelimer, the Vandal king, thought to have been situated near present-day Hammamet. Here, the soldiers were allowed to rest and pillage the fruit and they were amazed at such an abundance. The last thing Gelimer expected was this invasion and rapid advance on the part of Belisarius, for he was away at the old capital of Bulla Regia. Immediately he marched with his troops to confront Belisarius and encountered him some miles outside Carthage, but here he was decisively defeated on 15 September, St Cyprian's day. When Belisarius reached Carthage he sat down in the Palace and ate the meal that had been prepared for Gelimer. His action was not without precedent, for Julius Caesar had done the same thing after his victory at Dyrrhachium.

During the years of the Byzantine occupation the old towns were refortified against attack and the construction of the new walls often incorporated a great deal of material from the old Roman buildings. This at times included a triumphal arch. Many new churches and basilicas were built, the old pagan temples were consecrated and at this time Leptis itself was granted a new though short lease of life. What had lapsed under the Vandals was restored, but this activity in the sixth century meant that North Africa was heavily taxed; moreover, the schisms and heresies which opposed the Catholic doctrine were subjected to further persecution. The Berber tribes reverted to their own little hierarchies and the Byzantine local administration was not above reproach.

Justinian had by now sent Solomon, another of his generals, to Africa to replace Belisarius whom he had recalled in disgrace for having sat on the throne of Gaiseric after his defeat. The incident had been reported to Justinian in order to ferment his suspicions, for he had always been apprehensive lest he be dethroned. He took this act on the part of Belisarius, innocent though it was, as a sign of his intention to supplant him. Therefore, when Belisarius arrived in Constantinople he was stripped of his honours and fortune, a shabby reward and little thanks for the brilliant military successes which he had brought about for the good of the Empire. Robert Graves's book *Count Belisarius* gives a brilliant portrayal of the man and the events of the period. Justinian later on gave Sergius, a nephew of Solomon, the administration of Tripolitania, but all he managed to do was to stir up the Louata tribes with his massacres and oppressions and this led to more battles at Theveste and Cilium, and to the death of Solomon himself. The period that followed was once more one of continued unrest on the part of the Berbers; in a battle near Le Kef the Byzantines again lost the day again to the Louata tribe. Africa was now left subject to those militant armies that marauded the country until a decisive defeat was inflicted on the Berbers in the south by John Troglita, another of Justinian's able generals who had not long since arrived from Constantinople.

On the death of Justinian, Maurice became Emperor and gave the colonies more autonomy under their governors. Under his rule the Berber uprisings were not so serious, or so frequent. There had also been a good deal of unrest in the North African Church under Justinian, which now more or less ceased. However, even under Maurice, the poor inhabitants of the towns and those in the country were still subject to oppression, graft and corruption on the part of the government and they turned to the Church for solace and help. In their turn the bishops Dominicus of Carthage and Columbus of Nicivibus in Numidia sought the aid and support of Pope Gregory who, with the help of Hilarus who was his notary, imposed his administration on the African Church, which also was not above reproach. His personality was such that he also imposed his authority on the civil authorities, thus ensuring that corruption and oppression ceased to flourish. In AD 595, Maurice in Constantinople gave his foremost general, Heraclius, the administration of Africa, but whilst he was in office in Carthage the Emperor was murdered by Phocas, who usurped the Empire. In retaliation Heraclius witheld the corn supplies from Constantinople and sent his son, also called Heraclius, together with his nephew Nicetas, with troops to Constantinople to avenge Maurice and free his niece Eudocia, whom Phocas was holding as hostage. However, before they arrived, Phocas was killed in a revolt that had broken out in the capital, so that when Heraclius landed in AD 610 he found himself proclaimed Emperor, whereupon he married Eudocia.

Heraclius' reign lasted thirty years and was peaceful, though he did prevent the Persians under Chosroes from invading the country from the east. In North Africa even the Berbers were more co-operative and ceased their uprisings, but after his death dissent once again disrupted the African Church. This was chiefly due to the arrival of those who were fleeing from the Arab incursions in the east and they strove to convert the orthodox Catholics in Africa to their Monophysite heresies. It was back to square one again, only this time it was not the Donatists who were involved but the Catholics, against what they considered to be the heresy of Constantinople, and this led to their continued loyalty to the capital to fall into doubt.

It was the beginning of the end of Roman influence. Gregory, who had been appointed Governor of Carthage, declared himself Emperor in Africa in opposition to Constantinople, thus demonstrating North African independence and its final separation from the Byzantine

Empire. It was, however, short-lived. The Arabs were on their way. Muhammed the Prophet had died in Medina in AD 632, and in AD 641 the Arabs occupied Egypt, moving into Cyrenaica in AD 642 and on to Tripolitania the next year, where they devastated what was left of Sabratha. Gregory, who had declared himself Emperor in AD 546, moved his capital from Carthage to Sbeitla to meet the growing menace, but he died in its defence when his army was wiped out in AD 647 by Abdullah Ibn Saad.

The remaining Byzantines in the country bought fifteen years' respite from the victorious Arabs, but they returned under Oqba Ibn Nafi in AD 659 and swept in from the east to present-day Tunisia, where they founded and built the Holy City of Kairouan. Unfortunately for them there was a hitch in the invasion. The Berber tribes of Mauretania rose up against the advance and Oqba was ambushed and killed with most of his following near the oasis of Biskra in Algeria. It was a setback for the Arabs and their further attempts to establish themselves were thwarted by the Kahena tribes in the Aures mountains, named after their leader. She was a militant priestess, almost a Berber Boudica, who was joined by the few remaining Christians who had sought safety in the mountains.

The Arabs under Hassan returned in force in AD 698 and this time they entrenched themselves. For Roman Africa the fall of Carthage was the final curtain and the once dominant, but often bitterly opposed, Christian communities disappeared. Islam spread rapidly through the Berber tribes and crossed into Spain and spread almost to the Danube, but the Arabs were eventually pushed back to the African continent by Ferdinand and Isabella. The last town to fall was Rhonda in the mountains overlooking the Costa del Sol, but they left an indelible mark, especially with their art and architecture in the south of Spain.

However, Islam was to suffer the same conflicts and schisms that had befallen the Christian Church, dividing into the two main sects of Shia and Sunni. It was the Shias who evicted the Sunnis, those who acknowledged the Caliphate of Bagdad, from Kairouan in AD 909. Other smaller sects of Islam sprang up, like that of the Mozabites who inhabit the holy cities of the Zab in the Oasis of Ghardaia in southern Algeria. North Africa fared no better after the Arab Conquest than it did in Roman times, being subject to the same disputes, massacres, and tribal raids, but this is another story. It was ruled by the Turks from 1574 under a succession of Beys, who indulged in mass piracy and murder in the Mediterranean and built many of their present-day palaces and mosques on the proceeds. The French, in their turn, began their occupation in Algeria in 1830. The French Foreign Legion from fortified garrisons in the hinterland carried out the same functions that had befallen the lot of the Third Augustan Legion for over three hundred years. They also left a cultural heritage and a second language. It was during their occupation that many of the long forgotten cities were rediscovered, and unfortunately once again pillaged, before archaeology came to the rescue.

Visiting what is left of the towns in North Africa, deserted as they are, one must reflect on those of talent in literature and in law, and in other walks of life, who came from them and gave so much to the Roman Empire and to our present-day culture. There were those, of course, like Plautianus, who did not. One hopes that the final comment is not that which came from a sergeant of the Eighth Army, in a letter that he wrote home from Libya at the end of hostilities. He had attended a lecture (which one feels was compulsory!), given by the then Director of Army Education in Tripoli, who had become interested in the antiquities of Leptis and Sabratha. The sergeant wrote: 'We now know all about this place; it is full of the ruins of buildings put up by the Eyeties before the war, but as far as I can see, it is now just full of camels and Western Oriental Gentlemen!'.

Reigns of the Roman Emperors

27 BC—AD 14 Augustus
AD 14—AD 37 Tiberius
AD 37—AD 41 Caligula
AD 41—AD 54 Claudius
AD 54—AD 68 Nero
AD 68—AD 69 Galba
AD 69 Otho
AD 69 Vitellius
AD 69—AD 79 Vespasian
AD 78—AD 81 Titus
AD 81—AD 96 Domitian
AD 96—AD 98 Nerva
AD 98—AD 117 Trajan
AD 117—AD 138 Hadrian
AD 138—AD 161 Antoninus Pius
AD 161—AD 180 Marcus Aurelius
AD 161—AD 169 Lucius Verus, co-emperor
AD 178—AD 193 Commodus
AD 193 Pertinax
AD 193 Didius Julianus
AD 193—AD 211 Septimius Severus
AD 198—AD 217 Caracalla (198–211, co-emperor with Severus)
AD 209—AD 212 Geta, co-emperor with Severus and Caracalla
AD 211—AD 212 Geta, co-emperor with Caracalla after the death of Severus
AD 217—AD 218 Macrinus
AD 218—AD 222 Elagabulus
AD 222—AD 235 Severus Alexander; end of Severan Dynasty
AD 235—AD 238 Maximinus
AD 238—AD 284 Twenty short-lived emperors
AD 284—AD 305 Diocletian

Index